Saguisag Wit - 1

Rene Saguisag
(Compilation of Senator Saguisag writings)

Sept 21, 2016 – Aug. 9, 2018
(updated)

Saguisag Wit - 1

Published by

TATAY JOBO ELIZES.
Self-Publisher
in 2017, under the
permission and authorization of
RENE SAGUISAG

ISBN - 13: 978 - 1977629067
ISBN - 10: 1977629067

Contact: job_elizes@yahoo.com
Website: http://tinyurl.com/mj76ccq
www.tatayjoboelizes.webs.com

Special Note

Articles are arranged at random dates and appeared at The Manila Times and Worldwide Filipino Alliance Yahoo Group.

Contents

About the author – *p6*

ooooo

About the Author

Rene Saguisag *was born on August 14, 1939 in* <u>Mauban, Quezon,</u> *Philippines. Saguisag attended elementary school at Makati Elementary School in 1951 He graduated from* <u>Rizal High School</u> *in 1955*

Saguisag went on to graduate with a <u>Bachelor of Arts</u> *degree in 1959 from* <u>San Beda College</u>*. He also later graduated* <u>cum laude</u> *from San Beda College with a* <u>bachelor of laws</u> *degree in 1963 and placed 6th in the same year's* <u>Bar Examinations</u>*.*

Saguisag also obtained his Master of Laws degree from <u>Harvard University</u> *in 1968. Rene Saguisag practiced* <u>law</u> *as a prominent* <u>human rights lawyer</u> *in the Philippines from 1972 to 1986. He also became a spokesman for then president elect* <u>Corazon Aquino</u> *beginning on January 22, 1986. Saguisag was first elected to the* <u>Senate of the Philippines</u> *in 1987 He remained in the Senate until 1992. As a Senator, Saguisag served as chairman of the committee on* <u>ethics</u> *and* <u>privileges</u>*.* He was chairman of Senate committee on ad hoc committee on the Bataan Nuclear power plant and he was one of the two senators who attended all 415 session days from July 1987 to June 1990.

Senator Saguisag worked as a checker, laborer, construction site guard and messenger from 1959 to 1962. From 1962 to 1972 he became an student researcher, then associate and eventually part time in Ledesma, Guytingco, Velasco and Saguisag. He became a member,

Law Faculty (Assistant Dean 1971-1972) from 1961 to 1972. From 1972 to 1986 he practice law and a human rights lawyer. Senator Saguisag became the spokesman of candidate and president elect Cory Aquino from January 22, 1986.

He married Dulce Maramba Quintanas with whom he has four children.

Rene Saguisag practiced law as a prominent human rights lawyer in the Philippines from 1972 to 1986. He also became a spokesman for then president elect Corazon Aquinobeginning on January 22, 1986.

Rene Saguisag was one of only two Filipino Senators who attended all 415 session days from July 1987 to June 1990.[3]

Following his departure from the Senate, Saguisag became one of the leading defense lawyers in the corruption trial of former President Joseph Estrada.

Before President Estrada stepped down from Malacañang on account of the plunder case filed against him, right after the Philippine Centennial Celebration, Former Senator Rene Saguisag was appointed by Pres. Estrada to head the Ad Hoc and Independent Citizens' Committee (AHICC) with members Atty. Francis Pangilinan, Engr. Fiorello Estuar, USec. Antonio M. Llorente and Corazon dela Paz. AHICC was created by President Estrada on Feb. 24, 1999 through Administrative Order No. 53 to investigate if there were irregularities that transpired during the preparations and celebrations of Philippine Centennial Anniversary. AHICC found that the bidding for certain centennial projects had been rigged, that certain documents used in the bidding had been falsified, and that certain signatures on documents were forged.

Rene Saguisag was seriously injured in a <u>car crash</u> on November 8, 2007, in <u>Makati City</u>. A speeding <u>dump truck</u> struck Saguisag's van, killing his wife <u>Dulce Saguisag</u>, a former Secretary of the <u>Department of Social Welfare and Development</u>. Saguisag was left in <u>critical condition</u> following the collision. His injuries included seven broken <u>ribs</u> and small blood clots in his <u>brain</u>. However, his doctors stated that he had a "very good chance" of a full recovery. He spent 20 days in the <u>intensive-care unit</u>, and was released from the hospital on December 8, 2007.

Rene and Dulce's youngest daughter, Kaissa Saguisag is a <u>gymnast</u>, but a knee injury ended her quest for gold at the 24th <u>Southeast Asian Games</u> .[6]

Saguisag & Associates Lawyers 4045 Bigasan Street, Palanan 1235 Makati Office Nos. (+632) 551-6350/833-4140 Fax No. (+632) 831-2276. Email: ravslaw#gmail.com
c/o Manila times opinion
opinion@manilatimes.net

oooooo

Pictures

A SENADO

ooooooo

1

Di Po Pederalismo and Problema, Kundi Kayo Mismo

Aug 9, 2018

Senator Ping Lacson impishly said that his chamber is ready to cremate whatever Cha Cha cadaver the Bigger House may send to the Better House, Frankfurter&# 39;s "derelict upon the waters of the law" if I may mix my metaphors.

What made the Consultative Committee (Conscom) spokesman tap Mocha Uson to sell its Draft? That she could seduce the populace the way she apparently did candidate and now Prez

Digong? Was it because there is a CHA in her name, as in MO-CHA for CHA CHA?

"Ginoong Pangulo at Binibining Mocha, di po sistema ng pamahalaan ang problema, di po Pederalismo, kundi po, kayo mismo!"

A hard sell. She was reportedly approached to help lead the campaign to promote its Draft, on the initiative of the Conscom spokesman, who may or may not have clearance from it.

Permit me to doubt the wisdom of the move, validating that we are decaying in more than one front. Indeed, in what aspect of government are we better off today than we were when I was a law student and a young lawyer in the 50's and 60's? Are we a failed democracy?

It seems a truly serious YES campaign should be led by, among others, Chief Justice (CJ) Rey Puno, Senator Nene Pimentel, Vic de la Serna and Rudy Robles, topnotch lawyers; the latter three were elected ConCon Delegates in 1971. Fr. Rannie Aquino is a jurisprudence scholar or pundit.

But, what about the dismal aspect of economics?

Can they point to any tree with money growing on it?

In 1986-87, I, as Cory, Jr., was among those who led the campaign for the ratification of the Cory Constitution (now sought to be replaced by the Mo-CHA version). Walk in the park. But, it was the song, not the singer. Easy to sell the work of a body led by Justice Ka Celing Muñoz Palma as ConCom President, with Senator Ambo Padilla as Veep, aided by Chief Justice Berting

Concepcion, and many others whose patriotism and sagacity were beyond a peradventure.

Thereby was killed the 1973 Constitution. 1971 ConCon and 1986 ConCom Delegate Pepe Nolledo narrated that in 1973, Barangay Assemblies were supposedly held. Asked who wanted Siopao, the attendees raised their hands, which were then marked as Yes votes.

Manny Pacquiao, on the other hand, is pushing for the anti-poor death penalty. All the statistics show that the rich boy flies, the poor boy fries. Extrajudicially killed, the poor may now be judicially murdered. The law represents the biases of the ruling class. Manny should consider the poor from whose ranks he came.

Snake oil salespersons we seem to see all over.

Now comes my pal, Ferdie Topacio, a celebrity lawyer with a celebrity client I chanced upon last Monday in the Sandiganbayan cafeteria.

Ferdie, who flatters and flattens me by calling me Lodi, I again met the other evening in St. Luke's in the Fort. He was accompanying his ailing mother (not necessarily buying the facility). I learned about his presence because a waiter said he had picked up the tab, for us, unbidden.

Ferdie has helped put up a bounty for the heads of Ka Satur Ocampo, Liza Maza, Paeng Mariano and Teddy Casiño. The latter I met over dinner last July 24. I recall that Joker P. Arroyo would advise our detained national security clients, prisoners of conscience, that their first duty is to escape.

Ka Satur, et al., ingat, I don't know where any of you may be found; if I did, I ain't telling. But, if Ferdie raises the ante, I just might yield; Oscar Wilde said: "I can resist everything, except temptation."

Seriously, given that their alleged crime was supposedly committed about a dozen years ago, how I wish the Supreme Court could have found a way just to dismiss the case for the denial of the human and constitutional right to a speedy disposition of the case. So many years and not even first base we have reached, a very sad affirmation of Hamlet's "law' s delay." Inordinate delay indeed.

Lenny Villa was killed in an Aquila Legis hazing incident on February 11, 1991. Thanks to then Associate Justice Meilou Sereno, she finally decided the case on February 1, 2012. Among those acquitted was my client, Zos Dizon. On a motion for reconsideration, it was only in April 2016, when we got the ruling denying the motion, again, thanks to hardworking CJ Meilou. Actually, Zos, convicted by a Regional Trial Court, was acquitted twice by the Court of Appeals and twice by the Supreme Court! Multiple jeopardy and acquittals.

Going back to public hanging by the neck till dead, which the Prez prefers, what Manny Pacquiao should study is whether in its application, the death penalty has been anti-poor, the ranks from which he came. Taksil po sa kanyang kauri? **The rich criminals are probably in the corridors of power.**

The law represents the biases of the ruling class.

Manny and Tito Sotto should study the Portuguese experience and the UN General Assembly Special Session on Drugs. Portugal sees druggies as sick, who should be rehabbed, not as gun-grabbing criminals to be destroyed in our horrid prison system. By decriminalizing ALL drugs, the syndicates would wither and die, as government would supply the drugs. No rise in drug use in Portugal. In fact, it is going south.

Public hanging represents the best thinking of centuries ago. In England pickpockets would ply their trade while a hanging went on. We should not add judicial murder to extrajudicial killings. An eye for an eye, a tooth for a tooth, rape the rapist?*

Not only Manny Pacquiao has read the Bible. So also has the Pope. So have I, the Jerusalem Bible, cover to cover, from the Old Testament of Lamech, to Lex Talionis - to the New, which teaches compassion and forgiveness.

Do we prefer decay in values? Certainty and swiftness of conviction deter, not the severity of the penalty. A criminal does not carry a copy of the penal code and looks at what he can afford, a discredited supermarket theory of the criminal laws *> * Last Friday night, in a birthday party, someone sang Vincent (Starry Starry Night). Senator Vincent Sotto should play and listen to the
song with its haunting melody.

MABINI's Alex Padilla, of La Salle and UP, sang and danced in a party of Bedans whose BoyNing Suzara was marking a birth anniversary.

Bogs Bonifacio' s emailed invite had said Alex would sing MacArthur Park. He delivered. Bobby Mondejar, a friend of the bday boy, sang, with feeling, Vincent (Starry Starry Night), part of whose lyrics were emblazoned on a wreath in the wake of hero/martyr Dr. Bobby de la Paz in Malate in 1982. A few nights ago I watched on TV a film on Vincent Van Gogh's life. And very briefly last Tuesday early in the morning, MacArthur, starring Gregory Peck.

Dr. Sylvia was Dr. Bobby's widow I got to meet after my unsayable loss of 2007. The one we suspected to have been behind Bobby's salvaging, I got to know when my wife and I were dancexercising in Intercon. Col. F would wait in the coffee shop below and drank, while his wife also dancexercised in Bahia.

Music and dance have the power to make us happy in this vale of tears. Like meeting top showbiz types. Celebrities.

I met Joan Baez in Prez Cory's 1986 San Fran visit; earlier I met Sigourney Weaver in New York. In 1996, my wife and I saw Linda Ronstadt in Las Vegas and Blue Bayou alone was more than worth the cost of admission.

We need to relax to keep what is left of our sanity. "Now I understand what you tried to say to me, and how you suffered for your sanity, how you tried to set them free, they would not listen, they did not know how, perhaps they'll listen now, starry, starry night."

Here's hoping Digong and Mocha will listen to the people now.*

I cannot close without remarking that pepe I associate with Pepe and Pilar, Rizal, Nolledo and Ka Pepe Diokno, souls of decency. As a Tagalog only now am I told that it could be linked to toxic indecency. That's rich. Pekpek, let's stick with, and continue to link pepe with what is edifying. We all have a stake in arresting decay in values, institutions and processes certain administration types appear to want to continue leading us.

Saguisag & Associates Lawyers 4045 Bigasan Street, Palanan 1235 Makati Office Nos. (+632) 551-6350/833- 4140 Fax No. (+632) 831-2276.

ooooooo

2

TURBA SALVAJE ALL OVER

July 4, 2018

Turba Salvaje was an excellent local soccer team when I was young. Now we are nothing in today's gripping World Cup in Moscow. Our passion is in basketball, for which we aren't built.

Last Monday evening, I had dinner with a client, joined later by a son, Atty. Rebo, UAAP Executive Director. He had changed his mind about going to Bocaue and missed what he and I did: the embarrassing donnybrook between GILAS (should be SIGA? SIGALOT? TURBA SALVAJE?) and our guests from Down Under.

The first white settlers there were POMEs (Prisoners of Mother England) but the Aussies have since developed admirably high ethical standards, including shunning the Nazi salute of Hitler which Digong cherishes (fist bump).

There was no excuse for either side for the shameful melee; was our being so far behind a factor (we don't take defeats easily)? Do we include Manny Pacquiao in any future national team.(?) The PBA deems him good enough for the league as his billions speak but his Aussie conqueror, Jeff Horn, may also show up for a dream rematch.

Speaking of my son, I am asked from time to time if anyone among my children would go to politics to inaugurate my own dynasty. I have not encouraged the idea at all. Should I have?

In 1986, I worked in the Palace for P8,000.00 a month, as a member of the Cabinet. In the Senate later, my take-home pay was P14,612.50. But, I must agree with what they say in the U.S.: good people should go to the ministry/priesthood but the best ones should go to politics. So in politics and government, I (bilib sa sarile?) found myself, willy-nilly, from 1986 to 1992. How did I get there?

February 25, 1986, late afternoon, was unusual; we had two Presidents. I, spokesperson of candidate, Prez-elect and Prez Cory, was told by the Bosswoman that I'd continue to be her spokesperson! But, I had not planned to be in government! I was speechless, looking down at my shoes. I got chided, shanghaied and dragooned into saying yes, most reluctantly, by a piqued Prez who reminded me that I was among those who had persuaded her to run, "tapos, ngayon iiwanan mo ako"?

So I became an Accidental Public Servant helping a Providential President, from 1986 to 1992. I could not remain in politics however. Impatiently shunting aside any start of talk when she would say I should start considering higher office, and turning down a signed Supreme Court (SC) appointment in late January, 1987, some may say my head was not properly and tightly screwed on. A psycho, aren't I?

Flattering anyway was the Inquirer's articulate Joel Butuyan's column on me last Monday, on my walking away from power. Had I encouraged Prez Cory's overture, or had I accepted my SC posting, at 47, our history might have taken a different course, for better or for worse. But, I just was not cut out for life in government.

I continue to believe though that the best among us should go to government and not leave it to rapscallions. Still, one can serve without a title and without pay taken from the hide of the taxpayer.

Principled Joel's very kind piece spurred various positive reactions, including one from Gerry Tongco, who very kindly helped a teenaged girl convicted for kidnapping for ransom in 2005. He wrote Joel on how I "helped [him] help a poor woman languishing in jail for more than a decade. In 2011, I came across a case regarding a certain [Jean Doe] in the women's penitentiary in Mandaluyong. . . . [S]he was just 16 years old when the RTC convicted her and her companions of kidnapping [for ransom] and they were all sentenced to reclusion perpetua [death, in fact, then in force; life, for her, a minor]. . . .

"[S]entencing a minor to reclusion perpetua is truly a miscarriage of justice. To make the long story short, I approached Atty. Rene Saguisag. He did accept the case pro bono [puro abono, abonado, di abogado]. After 2 years, [the Supreme Court] set her free in October 2013 after being jailed for 17 years. If not for [Gerry and me] this poor lady [would have spent] her entire lifetime in jail. The last time I checked with her she got married and starting her life outside happily."

On appellate correction. Justice Vicente Veloso (quo warranto originator, rendering Chief Justice Sereno jobless but, providentially, not having been impeached and convicted, makes her eligible to run as Senator), in People v. Padilla, CA G.R. No. CR. 22349, the magistrate, now a Congressman, acquitted my client in 2004; also acquitted was Rommel Padilla, a brother of Robin, who our San Beda alum, Robert - whew, another Padilla - represented, with Philip Jurado (who the Prez baselessly, unkindly and unfairly named and shamed).

Robin has many siblings; the lore, maybe apocryphal, that circulated in 1986 was, Prez Cory said, "Roy," (a Bicol Governor, father of the Padillas, legendary Kamandags), "I am sorry but I cannot proceed with your appointment as Minister of Labor." Roy, her first choice, stunned, asked: "But, why po, Ma'm?" Prez Cory: "Cuz I understand you have 57 children." Roy: "Ma'm, 43 lang po."

Early this millennium, coming from ballroom dancing, past midnight, Robin called and asked that I proceed to Medical Center Manila (MCM) to assist his Muslim driver tending to his preggy wife. The driver, charged with some offense, was to surrender in Camp Crame, where we went at the crack of dawn, with Karen Davila.

Robert and Digong belong to SBC's law class of 1972, which was when the latter shot a classmate, Octavio Goco, for labelling him a promdi. Digong has said his first kill was in a teenage rumble. Joke?

Of course Digong is entitled to his opinion on religion. No question. But, to express it, to divide, not to unite, to add pain, and not to share ours, is something else. He should heal wounds, not exacerbate same, which should be left to his attack dogs, if at all.

It disappoints that Digong who attended Ateneo and San Beda could say God is stupid and not apologize. If he had simply said "sorry," or "just joking," we could all have put the matter behind us. But, overweening false pride prevents him from doing the right thing in the country's best interests. And so our decay in values continues (good that after the Bocaue basketbrawl, prompt apologies galore).

He is our No. 1 Role Model, seen as father of the nation.

I spoke against Tanauan, Batangas Mayor Tony Halili's** Walk of Shame, parading and shaming of druggies - presumed to be innocent - but if the Prez and the PDEA had evidence of drug links, Hizzoner was entitled to due process.

When Henry II blurted, "will no one rid me of this turbulent priest?," four Knights considered themselves told and sent the Canterbury Archbishop to paradise. The Prez must realize the powerful effect of his rhetoric on human conduct.

Let us hope that the planned Palace-Church dialogue will calm the Palace-induced turbulence that conduces to the murder of priests, mayors and the poorest of the poor.

There's a new turba salvaje among scalawags or vigilantes.

oooooo

3

STUPID GOD(S)?

Jun 28, 2018

As a Makati Elementary School grader, I found June 29 - like today - special. Feast of San Pedro at San Pablo. Big day in San Pedro, Makati. One joy was in the peryahan in the ample front yard then (now super-cramped) of the church in Poblacion. There I gambled. Terembe. Pula Puti. Atbp.

I do not gamble today. The wealthy do, in casinos, horse racing, cockfight derbies, etc. Legally - while the poor cannot bet in jueteng. But, gambling is in our DNA; the Pinoy would bet on anything that moves. I support Digong's reported proposal to legalize and tax jueteng. I find it invidiously discriminatory that the rich can gamble in casinos, cockfights and horse racing while the poor cannot bet in jueteng.

Manny Pacquiao can, in cockfights. The billionaire boxer who sees Senatoring as child's play, insists that his fight with wassisname Matthysse is on. But, I wonder how many would watch the fight in, of all places, Malaysia. Sounds like scraping the bottom of the barrel. Muhammad Ali is the only prominent Muslim I can think of in the Manly Art of Modified Murder. OK, Mike Tyson also converted (Malik Abdul Aziz).

Time, Senator Manny, to retire and stop making the Senate look bad as a part-time chore, sideline or hobby. With Senate Prez Tito Sotto perceived or misperceived as another Digong fanatic or lemming, what else does Digong not control in government? And what does Preacher Manny think of "God is stupid" ? But, "do not disturb" ?? However, vocal opposition is needed in a democracy for positive creative tension. "Dialogue" ; could lead to "daya na, lugue pa," in our experience.

I was nearly catatonic hearing the Prez says my God - omigod! – is "stupid."

Imagine a new Constitution with a Preamble saying "imploring the aid of a Stupid God. . . ." The Prez's fascinating Constitutional Commission has its work cut out for it. (Budget Secretary Ben Diokno has to tell us how much the body has cost us so far; the Prez can totally ignore its work, a derelict in the waters of the law, the brilliance, patriotism and piety of certain members notwithstanding.)

After years of Benedictine piety and a bit of Jesuitical casuistry for the Prez, here we are, with a Stupid God, in his view.

Wotta great blasphemy! - Benedictine Father Urbano Casares would boom in the Church of Our Lady of Montserrat when I was in pre-law, in the finest law school along the entire length and breadth of Mendiola (which the Prez was to attend about a decade or so later, and whose teachings on God he has arguably rejected). No Fr. Casares today?

We, Christians, et al., are advised to be meek and turn the other cheek but certain hard-core Muslims just might take offense if anyone called Allah "stupid, " the comical terminological jiu-jitsus of Digong's mouthpieces notwithstanding. Remember Salman Rushdie and fatwa. And, in a proper case, Onward, Christians Soldiers. . . .

We need to speak up. So I have urged the Benedictine community, that our fellow Bedan may walk back, for everyone' s sake. Some of the cruelest lies are often told in silence. - Robert Louis Stevenson.

We don't want anyone taking an oath and ending with "So help me, Stupid God." Good manners and right conduct matter.

Of course there are the gods of Padre Faura. Maybe the spin could be that Digong was alluding to one of the stupid dissenting six (Justice TonyCarp deserves to be elevated, notwithstanding) . Those for judicial indepen-dence may have in mind the stupid majoritarian eight. Democracy.

In the choice of a new Chief Justice (CJ), we see a number of names to be considered. The Judicial & Bar Council even invites nominees; I see no requirement of seniority for CJ but Senior TonyCarp is a shoo-in, in my book. However, nominees now in government have to remember the Veloso-Mallari-Calida test, as it were. It was Cong. Alberto Veloso, a former Court of Appeals Justice - who I sorta remember for penning the 2004 reversal of a Pasig Regional Trial Court decision convicting my client below, which we appealed successfully, thanks to him - who first mentioned Quo Warranto.

Compañero Eligio Malari and SolGen Joe Calida picked it up and Joe told the Supreme Court in bold in his QW petition (page 28) that R.A. No. 3019 required CJ Meilou to file a statement which includes income earned, expenses incurred and taxes paid. So, the JBC should verify whether any CJ applicant has so complied. No one will pass the Veloso-Calida-Mallari test, not even TonyCarp, I am afraid. Nor the JBC members. But, I do not see it as a disqualifying measure of integrity in our scofflaw society.

I remain uncomfortable with having to apply for an appointment as judge, as Chief Justice, more so. Roberto Concepcion and JBL Reyes applying to be appointed or promoted? Susmariano! When I was young, cream would simply rise to the top. Then Marcos came and damaged our values. Processes and institutions, like the judiciary (there was a short-lived renaissance in 1986, I like to think). Declining, not applying, TonyCarp should be appointed; the post should be thrust on him.

No, Justice Tony, don't fight it. It is your Destiny.

Whether to retain the Judicial & Bar Council and return to the Commission on Appointments has to be studied carefully. We need to arrest decay where only certain hard-line godless Communists would not mind God being called stupid by our No. 1 citizen, seen as a role model, no ordinary Juan de la Cruz with no vast influence. Digong has to exercise his right not to speak more often. He has attack dogs to do the dirty job. He has to change, for our sake. He has to be, well, prudent naman sana.

Inday Sara advises not to mind him but offending the religious feelings of the faithful is an affront not easy to ignore.

One change I see, on top of worse traffic, is that the status of peace and order has so deteriorated that for the first time in memory, there is a debate on whether or not to arm priests of a Church with "stupid" teachings. And so would be Barangay officials (before, one became Tininti del Baryo through sheer prestige until the Pelaez Law took effect when I was a law senior and got elected as a Barrio Councilor, willy-nilly).

Ngayon di daw po sinabi ni Digong na arestohin ang mga tambay. Susmariano! Nakakahilo. Sino po ngayon ang mga gago? Di po ba mga pulis na hindi maunawaan ang simpleng utos ng palamurang Pangulo? Again, to be a bum harming no one is a human and constitutional right, in my view, and experience.

I was also a bum, a tambay, in my time, in Pasig, in the kanto sari-sari store of affable Chino Pio, and later, in the town plaza, where our barkada made sure Rizal's monument was not stolen. At times, we would have post-midnight snacks in the palengke, with steaming rice, using our washed hands (kamayan), and even join viajeros buying livestock and fruits in Batangas. We enjoyed our right to be let and left alone.

Today I may be accosted/arrested? Or "rescued"?

Are we really decaying? Have we gone far in the wrong direction? Reverse, reverse, I plead, on bended knees.

On July 2, happy birthday, Madama Meldy and CJ Meilou, who may be a Senator on her 59th natal anniversary in 2019, and help provide constructive opposition, for everyone' s sake, in a seeming wrecking-ball administration.

ooooooo

4

TRAGEDY OF ERRORS; REMEMBERING HEROES

Jun 20, 2018

Last Tuesday, Chief Justice (CJ) Meilou was made to join, willy-nilly, the ranks of eleven million jobless Pinoys, as it were. She fell, again I say, into the arms of her people. She has more than proven her point, beyond a peradventure. The Prez bellowed he wanted her, his enemy, removed. Done.

But, the generally genuflectory Supreme Court failed to rule unanimously, unlike in the U.S. segregation case in 1954, the ruling against Nixon in 1974 (surrender of the Watergate tapes), and the decision against Tsikboy Clinton in 1997 (no presidential immunity); unanimous, and thus gained easy acceptance. The Justices there in Washington, D.C. are otherwise seen as nine scorpions in a bottle.

Here, we had a close vote, 8-6, which would have been 8-7 if the CJ had not shown the class several colleagues had checked at the door. Had she voted, it would have been 8-7.

In paraphrase, may I say that doubtless, certain high feelings of the moment will be satisfied but in the sober afterglow may come the realization of the sad implications of the extra slim majority decision. History will decide. Ultimately.

For another arguable error, elsewhere, the seemingly indolent Palace apparently committed another grave error by calling Roilo Golez - Rogelio, now in his grave. A netizen emailed me that he had gone to Roy's wake: he said: "I went to the wake of Roilo (coined from ROmblon and ILOilo) at Heritage Park" and met Vice Mayor Rico Golez, in "very ordinary clothing, a humble person." Fruit does not roll far from the tree. I hope humble Roy's heroism is not soon forgotten.

We may otherwise be too forgetful.

When I was a Makati Elementary grader, we'd sing "for Rizal was born on June 19, . . ." which seems to be hardly marked in this day and age (our paper, the best in town, did remember and front-paged a pix of a sculpture of the hero last Tuesday). It was a haunting melody but I am not aware, and doubt, that it is still sung today. We seem to have a shallow sense of history as well as shifting values.

Cory Benipayo Mojica reminded me that today, June 22, would have been the 98th birth anniversary of Ka Jovy Salonga had he lived, in a country run like heaven - or hell - depending on where one is (nakikinabang o inaaapi or just as a citizen Juan in the middle of the road, where most accidents happen).

I was raised to call him Uncle. His mother (Lola Dinang) and my own Lola (Ka Talia) were first cousins, living in the same Barrio San Miguel, Pasig looban. As my Lola was barren of milk, Daddy had to suck from the breasts of wet-nurse Lola Dinang, so we were told.

I had known Uncle Jovy only from afar then. I had no yen for politics. But, martial law eventually drew us closer, sharing a passion for human rights and constitutionalism, out of fashion today.

Prima Cory BM above echoed many others in saying that "[p]erhaps in this era of foul-mouthed, ill-mannered, uncouth government officials, columnists like [me] should take this opportunity to write about another era when this Statesman, Congressman, three-time topnotch Senator and Senate President set the bar for being a Strong Christian (not a Strong Man in this day's connotation) ." She added: "[I was] one of those who knew him best - at work [in the Better House] and at one-on-one interaction. Perhaps a feature on him will inspire a more gentlemanly code of conduct and integrity in true governance and public service." Sana naman, although it may be a Sisyphean enterprise or undertaking at this time of Hitler's Nazi salute being popularized by the Prez, all over, with uninformed or terrorized guests aping him.

I note also that there was hardly any mention last week of the Battle of Bessang Pass of June 14-15, 1945, when my friend and San Beda Law faculty colleague, Desi Jurado, helped break the backbone of Japanese resistance. Desi helped free us from foreign invaders but, sadly, not from our very own dictators. When last we met in Quezon City in the 70's or 80's, he urged us to keep going, in MABINI, and with a wistful faraway look, wondered aloud about whatever happened to that young man who once upon a time was ready to give his all for the Motherland. He had done more than enough.

And now, his son Rudolf Philip Jurado, honest and competent, was kicked around, named, shamed and ridiculed, by our current intolerant virtual dictator, who even cussed him in public, without bothering to get his side of the story. He deserved due process. Everybody does.

Father Desi had led a maneuver and lost a number of his men in Bessang Pass and now he may be said to have lost again, rolling in his grave at the grave injustice done to a son. Today, in the Libingan ng Mga Bayani is a fake hero, Macoy, who claimed to be in Bessang Pass, when in fact he was hundreds of kilometers away. Aside from Desi, we should remember Calixto Duque, Conrado Rigor, et al..

If we must mark our defeats, like those in Bataan and Corregidor, there must be a day for Bessang Pass, to mark one great Filipino victory. I support the proposal to declare June 14, 1945 a holiday, at least regionally, if not nationally.

BTW, Uncle Jovy himself was captured in April 1942 and was tortured, sentenced to 15 years of hard labor, but was pardoned on Japan's Foundation Day in 1943 and he co-topped the bar with Ka Pepe Diokno in 1944 with 95.3%. Not enough has been done either to mark the sterling sacrifice of Chief Justice Pedro Abad Santos of a worthy Supreme Court, executed in Lanao on May 2, 1942, for refusing to collaborate with the invaders. He could have gone to Australia and then the U.S., to be part of our government in exile, but chose to stay with his suffering people.

Did our heroes sacrifice in vain?

Today, we are a country which even sees as criminal the constitutional right to be a bum, with eleven million unemployed. Veep Leni Robredo, I see, points out that R.A. No. 10158 of 2012 decriminalized vacancy under Art. 101 of the Revised Penal Code. But, the cops always obey the Malacañang Lawgiver. And it seems they enforce local ordinances but it seems to me Congress has preempted the field of vagrancy and cannot be thwarted and sidestepped below.

I do hope however that we can deter our tambays from going around half-naked; fully naked may present another set of problems, depending on sex, age, etc. and the fact that UP has its annual "oblation run," with no reported prosecution. "Tradition? " But, Art. 11 of the Civil Code says: "Customs which are contrary to law, public order or public policy shall not be countenanced. " A tradition has been defined in Spain as a social vice that has become incurable (un vicio social que se ha vuelto incurable).

One vice I see is Protectee Digong and his mouthpieces acting as China's spokesmen. Protector China can speak for itself, surely. We should also speak up, in tribute to our heroes like Jose Rizal, Roy, Uncle Jovy, Desi, et al. who, oppressed, resisted and meant it when they sang "ang mamatay ng dahil sa 'yo" -emblazoned in their hearts.

After two years, I hope our President has acquired the security and confidence to be humble. I hope he also learns why "distinguished diplomat Delia Albert," per Malaya Business Insight' s gutsy Ellen Tordesillas the other day "stood out because she was the only one who was not doing the idiotic fist pump which has become the signature gesture of Duterte and his sycophants." She added: "Oh, Sen. Loren Legarda was . . . not doing the fist pump in the picture," either.

Leila de Lima, Chit Carpio-Morales, Meilou Sereno, Delia Albert, Loren Legarda, and other women inspire hope and help arrest our decay, as we await the wisdom of a new day.

Here, I note the wisdom and heroism now of Justice TonyCarp, who is not interested in becoming the next CJ. Revered Justice JBL Reyes never became CJ (and I may say good morning to myself, in January 1987, I myself, at 47, turned down a signed Supreme Court appointment and life went on; we can do so much more with less obsession for recognition).

Saguisag & Associates Lawyers 4045 Bigasan Street, Palanan 1235 Makati Office Nos. (+632) 551-6350/833- 4140 Fax No. (+632) 831-2276

oooooo

5

DENGXAVIA, APPEASEMENT AND ROY GOLEZ
Jun 13, 2018

In my mind's eye, I see Mengke Bateer, nearly seven feet tall, reportedly a pure Chinese Inner Mongolian who played in the NBA. It is a question whether such distinction can be said of any pure Pinoy. Anyway, a country more associated here with barbecue spanked our 3x3 team in basketball, where we continue to fantasize we can compete with the world's best (when in fact those not good enough for the NBA come here). Bateer belongs to the race of Yellows, a color now unkindly derided hereabouts.

Reading a citizen' s letter to the Inquirer editor printed last Monday ("Aquino is culpable" for Dengxavia), were I not an incorrigible Yellowtard, I would have seen, again with my mind's eye, PNoy sitting down with Executive Secretary Butch Abad, Health Secretary Janette Garin, and Sanofi, plotting on how to knock off dozens of children as part of some bizarre population reduction program. Then the new administration, in equal bad faith, picked up and continued the blameworthy program.(?)Absurd.

For judgment calls, made in good faith, which is presumed, Presidents answer to history, not to any court. Perfection is not a requirement to be President. Infallibility may be ascribed to Popes, in a very limited sense. And Alexander Pope wrote, to err is human, to forgive, divine.

Thus, we may not charge President Duterte for his puzzling policy of arguably pusillanimous appeasement vis-a-vis China. History will decide if his policy of national survival is superior to firm resistance to the new Yellow Peril we see. Or will he be our Neville Chamberlain appeasing Hitler?

Sad to note that last Monday Movement and Alliance Against China (MARCHA) leader Roilo Golez left this "wala-tayong- magagawang-mga-busabos"; nation.

I will always remember him. of a certain time in a certain way. Enlightened Roy was the first senior official of the Marcos regime I recall boldly joining the People at Edsa on February 22, 1986, an electrifying decision over Radio Veritas that sounded like he'd rather die on his feet (with the trapped putschists, later to be protected and rescued eventually by the People ready to die for the Motherland), than live in shame on bended knees. Early that evening, Roy went to Camp Aguinaldo to stake his all with the beleaguered plotters Malacañang could barbecue any moment. A leader, by example.

He had been the stellar Postmaster General of Marcos and around the time of his defection rumor was rife that a number of us openly opposed to Marcos were listed as targets in some Operation Mad Dog roster. Assemblyman Louie Villafuerte, in one frantic crucial meeting after February 22 warned against "one last act of madness" of the regime, in a meeting presided over by Ka Tanny Tañada and Ka Celing Muñoz-Palma.

Thank you Roy and Godspeed.

The one word in English that says it all, per St. Loo star pitcher Joaquin Andujar, is you-never-know, as when the saints or whoever would go marching in. Roy was 71 and not known - not to me anyway - to be ailing. I am 78. Prez Digong is 73.

Mayor Sara has announced that she would like to join her Tsikboy Tatay in his foreign trips to ride shotgun and avoid a repeat of the Seoul incident. It seems she does not approve of his father's osculatory tendencies. My take is if the Korean hubby and his family didn't mind, should we? Unless we fret about the continuing decline and decay in values.

Ubiquitous Special Assistant to the President (SAP) Bong Go emerges a winner in the Seoul "kiss is still a kiss" episode as Kris Aquino said she would campaign for him in his Senate run, an after-effect of her cat-fight with Mocha Uson. He denies having any senatorial dream or fantasy but I am reminded of what Times columnist Joe Guevara wrote about a

President saying "I will not run for reelection." Then, "I will not run." And finally, "I will." Hence, the observation that one can tell when most traditional politicians lie, their lips move.

Mayor Sara, likewise mentioned for the Senate along with Kris, Mocha Uson and Meilou Sereno. also has to deal with the SALN inquiry into a brother' s filings. As a co-author and floor sponsor of R.A. No. 6713 in the Senate, may I repeat my purely personal - and arguably erroneous - insight that the intent of the law is more administrative than criminal. Hence, a review and compliance procedure, to be complied with before any administrative or punitive action is taken.

SolGen Joe Calida hammered in his quo warranto petition, in bold even, that a public servant must report his income earned, expenses incurred and taxes paid. I have a copy of his latest filing; he himself did not comply. Neither has the Prez in his 2017 filing (I have no copy yet of his 2018 filing). I doubt that anyone in government has complied with Sec. 7 of R.A. No. 3019, the 1960 anti-graft law of Sen. Turing Tolentino. I also dispute that we can argue then that no one in government has integrity. Certainly, non-compliance does not rise to an impeachable level. All in government are requested to read Sec. 7 the SolGen quote, and measure their own integrity by it. I fear all would fail that hyped overblown test. All government personnel would have to go.

In this regard, may we see the SALNs of the members of the Presidential Anti-Crime Commission whose creation may be unconstitutional and which duplicates the work of other trained, established offices.

Coming back to appeasement, I see that the Senate would probe the landing of a Chinese military aircraft in Davao, to refuel kuno. We need to know where it came from and where it would fly to need to refuel. And why Davao? Why not Clark, Manila or Mactan? May China land and fish and build military facilities anywhere they want in our territory it seems to consider its own? We need answers to these foolish questions during this week of kasarinlan or Independence.

Recall how one may tell a trapo is lying: his lips move. But. one could simply be mistaken. Such as in continuing to ascribe to Raul Manglapus what many others had said earlier, including Confucius, who counselled that if rape is inevitable, just lie back and enjoy it.

Here, we seem to have found fair Laetitia's solution to prevent her rape by Fireblood - giving her timely consent.

Are we just going to lie back and enjoy it? Smart? Or idiotic?

Boracay earns millions of foreign exchange as a world-class resort. Do the natives there really want to agrarian-reform it to produce world-class camote? Smart? Or idiotic?

What is welcome to the human rights community is PNP Chief Oscar Albayalde's decision of not presenting suspects to media, to mitigate Digong's sorry name-and-shame malpractice. Digong is now quoted to have said reportedly that someone would shoot Senator Sonny Trillanes. Henry II asked "who will rid me of this boisterous priest?" Four knights considered themselves told and sent Archbishop Thomas Becket to the Promised Land.

oooooo

6

PHILIP J, FLORIN H, AND JOE C, ON ALLOWANCES, ETC.

Jun 6, 2018

We do have the Universal Declaration of Human Rights, not to be trumped by any Parochial Declaration of a leader like Meyor (his preference) Digong, our Kissing Bandit, who just validated what Henry Kissinger said: power is a great aphrodisiac. One in power is pogi, fires up hormones and fantasizes he is Heaven's gift to women. The song, As Time Goes By, in Casablanca, says, "A kiss is still a kiss," but if the hubby and his family don't complain, maybe we shouldn't either.

Anyway, the Bandit tells UN official Diego Garcia Sayan to "go to hell." Fellow Tsikboy Quezon did say he preferred a government run like hell by Pinoys to one run like heaven by Kanos. So a promotional stunt then???

Welcome to our shores. Dan Brown did call Manila as "the gates of hell" in Inferno (2013).

What about a government run like heaven by China? The Chinese are said to be driving up the cost of condominiums. My late wife would tell me how it was to bargain in Divisoria with sellers able to speak only pidgin Tagalog. So the cellphone would do. My late Mom would tell me about how Lola ran a boarding house in Mauban for Japanese renters who turned out to be advance men for the invaders.

In the 40's and 50's, one could hear in my youth about how rich men entered public life and left it poor. Macoy was a game-changer.

SolGen Joe Calida has a perceptual problem in having hundreds of millions worth of contracts with the government. It may not do to say his wife is running the business. We Manila Imperialists use the term "nag-iisang dibdib," which should apply to public officials. For Davao Imperialist SolGen Joe to say that it is his wife's business may not fly because husband and wife are one in more ways than one. Look at how Digong's cronies rise in wealth. "It' s still the same old story, the fight for [pelf] and glory. . . ."

But, are the Calidas really one? A Triangle we hear. A sweet young thing getting P1.8M of purported public funds.?(?)?

A probe is needed to see if he has the Digong Syndrome. Digong hollers for a pay increase for his two "wives" (let alone his kulasisis). That may be why he is understanding as to Joe who is said to have given P1.8M to keep his supposed 22-year-old GF in the OSG happy. Did his wife create a scene in his office cuz of his philandering (not necessarily plundering)?

That Joe's predecessor, highly regarded Florin Hilbay also had allowances may not be enough justification. (Mr. and Mrs. Wong, separated for a year, had Mr. coming home, and was shown a new Caucasian baby. He sued for divorce alleging that two Wongs can't make a white.) If we are talking of petty cash, say fishball, Walkman or IUD money on the sidewalks of Amorsolo St., in Makati, free pass maybe.

But P750T is much too much; we deal not with decrees, statutes or executive issuances. Chief Justice (CJ) John Marshall said: "it is a Constitution we are expounding" (1819). Sec. 24 of Art. VI of our Constitution says an appropriation bill can originate exclusively in the elected House, to be concurred in by the elected Senate, which trumps mere statutes or decrees, more so, issuances of the unelected. Congress, caponized by the Supreme Court (SC) in removing CJ Sereno, should take alarm at this further experimentation with the power of the purse. Indeed, the SC should have asked the Senate to be joined as an indispensable party in the Quo Warranto (QW) case; its power to remove impeachable official could be minimized. As it happened, it was.

CJ Meilou could have given his side of the story in the Senate, the proper institutional arrangement, in my view. Deprived of that by the slowpoke House, the SC should be more tolerant of her direct appeal to the particles of popular sovereignty, the people. It should be able to thrive in a hardy climate. And it should do do something about leaks. Now 16th Justice Jomar Canlas - not SolGen Joe who spreads his superstition - foretold last Monday the fate of CJ Meilou's motion for reconsideration.. Di po bulaang propeta si Jomar.

More fiscal abuse. A new Senate building in the Fort? I have my reservations and concerns; it will continue the anomaly of two chambers being far apart, conducing to friction and inefficiency. The billions could be spent for a new national penitentiary in say, Tanay, and the House and Senate can both move to Munti(for one term in office, one term in jail.)

If the U.S. is the model, I know the two chambers are near each other. I had trained in Washington DC's Arnold & Porter and would occasionally go to the Capitol (and returned with a triumphant Prez Cory in September 1986). Hungary' s Parliament, a model? But its legislature is unicameral. A concern is we are now, or may return to, zerocameral, as in 1972. No allowances issue.

Early last month Philip Jurado tried to curb Office of the Government Counsel Corporate Counsel allowances and got fired, named and shamed publicly by the Prez for his effort. He is the son of authentic Bessang Pass hero Desiderio Jurado, who fought for country, decency and due process denied Philip by a new Emperor, from Davao. Philip deserved due process, not cusses. For turning down allowances, he was arguably intrigued out of office. (Now, Boholana Philhealth chief Jude de la Serna, fired qua chief also without due process; she must be related to my campus contempo, ex-Tsikboy Vic de la Serna, 1965 Bar No. 1, now a member of Digong's Constitutional Commission, who could have explained well why her expenses were justified; she had to commute from Bohol to Manila, where she stayed in modest lodging units, not having a home in the nation's capital. How much has Digong spent/wasted in going to and from Davao?

CJ Meilou could have given her side in the Senate impeachment trial, the mode picked by six Justices. Thereby, the sovereign people, through their ELECTED Congressmen and Senators, would have been heard and would have decided, rather than fifteen UNELECTED Justices, some with publicized animus towards her. It seems to me impeachment is the far superior institutional arrangement. She has a very able and articulate supporter in former Solgen Hilbay. He is on the same page with SolGen Calida on allowances, which puzzles. Reliance on presidential decrees and statutes which cannot trump the Constitution which says only in the House can originate the disbursement of public money - seems misplaced. Giving modest allowances may deserve a free pass, but humongous sums without congressional involvement?

Of course it may be only me, not at par with Bar Topnotcher Florin (No. 1), which most everyone in the profession knows, or with SolGen Joe who reminds everyone and his mother he got 100% in criminal law in the bar exams; Joe possibly reported in his latest filing how much he earned, from all sources, how much he spent for personal and family needs, and the taxes he paid last year, he had demanded of CJ Meilou. Permit me to doubt, given my copy of his latest SALN, given me by a stude. House SALNS, para daw pong humihila ng bayawak sa lungga.

Joe had admirably and correctly pointed out on pages 28-29 of his remarkable QW petition that Sec. 7 of R.A. No. 3019, a penal law in which he says he is an expert, requires such disclosure which he and Digong ignore (I have copies of their elliptical filings but I would not say that their failure to comply with Sec. 7 of the Tolentino law bespeaks lack of integrity, without more. Shortcoming is far from wrongdoing.)

But, may anyone in government get P7.5M in allowances on top of this pay and other perks without involving Congress?

Same problem I have with the Presidential Anti-Crime Commission (PACC). In our scofflaw society, an ad hoc panel I can abide but another seemingly permanent investigating agency requiring millions? It would only be another attack dog of the Prez, not content with the Office of the Ombudsman, Department of Justice, the NBI, and the Criminal Detection and Investigation Group. Aside from the costs, the agencies may come up with contrasting findings like ships passing one another on a dark moonless night. I humbly question the legality of the existence of PACC - my foolish question of the day in a whatever-Lolo- D-wants Lolo- D-gets culture. Let us see if the PACC would probe the SolGen's alleged romancing a 22-year-old maiden and what he needs humongous allowances for. The Prez should always take and stick to the high road.

Do we still have decency and the Rule of Law? Or we are now in the Third Stage of Savagery, Civilization and Decay? We have to soldier on and not lose our moral stamina in helping a Kissing Bandit find his way, as in wage increase, a road not taken by the Prez, who showed class with Senator-to-be Bong Go in apologizing to Kris Aquino?.

Populist wage increase demanded by organized labor is tricky as it does nothing for our unemployed eleven million, who are unorganized, a constituency with no district or party list representation. The 11,000,000 live in life's Red Light Districts, as it were, of our communities, such as where I live, in Palanan, Makati. NPAs, No Permanent Addresses, estero and sidewalk dwellers in their tiny places in the sun. We need more land. "No Philippine territory lost under Duterte?" But, unconstitutional Chinese military facilities are reported to be in what we own.

We are losing by default. In the first Warriors-Cavaliers game a rhubarb on the "restricted area" arose. Our territory is a "restricted area" for alien military facilities under Sec. 25 of Art. XVIII, of the 1987 Constitution which creative China Protectee and Kissing Bandit Digong seems to ignore. Is there no Gurkha strain in this administration, to remind and rally us that we should prefer to die on our feet than live in shame on bended knees?

Saguisag & Associates Lawyers4045 Bigasan Street, Palanan1235 MakatiOffice Nos. (+632) 551-6350/833- 4140 Fax No. (+632) 831-2276

oooooo

7

LENI DEFENDED; TANNY REMEMBERED

May 30, 2018

Latest on Veep Leni Robredo in this misogynistic administration is the rehashed tsismis indicating worsening Truth Decay in that she supposedly has a BF, a Congressman, with whom she is seen. Leni I met in the Bantayog ng mga Bayani, on November 30, 2016, National Heroes Day. Last Sunday, it was Chief Justice (CJ) Meilou Sereno - so serene - I met in the same venue, for the rites to mark another anniversary of the passage of Senator Lorenzo M. Tañada, Sr. (Ka Tanny) in 1992.

Leni has repeatedly credibly denied the yarn made up of whole cloth, and explains away the Congressman concerned' s presence as a Liberal Party matter. Good enough for me, coming from my 2013 ex-San Beda grad law school stude. (Elected to Congress, she understandably quit.)

Her being relatively young and attractive she cannot help. But, I suppose her vow was not only "till death to us part" but beyond. Very much like mine so I should have remained above suspicion myself. But, I recall telling my Dulce, "dear, if you go ahead, I won't look at another woman again." Said she: "Hu, nakaburol pa lang ako. . . ." Said I: "Ang sakit mo namang magsalita, siempre intayin ko namang matapos ang burol.

" Sabay ilag. (As it happened, I was in ICU for weeks, no chance for a final hug, "goodbye, thank you and I'm sorry." But, God's will and I am accepting. While I felt like I had lost My Everything, my apos - oldest, 9 - with her long piliks serve as my Dulce Consuelo, her full name.)

Suppose we inaugurate some intrigue on why seemingly inseparable Digong and Bong Go are always together? No takers? Likely, just a transparent Senate seat campaign pa-pogi tactic (no passion for anonymity, unlike FPJ, who helped and donated, unadvertised) . In 2016, Digong said he and Sonny Dominguez - et tu, Sonny? - would ogle Leni's gams in Cabinet meetings. (Presidents may be the leading tsismosos in our sick society.. In our time in Malacañang, all kinds of tsismis would reach us.) Good, Leni left the Cabinet led by oglers in their second adolescence so it could get some work done. Secretary Berna, kudos, but always wear long pants or slacks. Loverly, cuz maganda ang Nanay, Lovely sorry, Manong Bert.

Anyway, very early last Saturday morning, a branch of the huge Tañada clan got me at 6:30 to take me to Bantayog ng Mga Bayani to help mark another death anniversary of the Grand Old Man.

Fr. Robert Reyes said Mass. To my left was Cong. Raul Daza. To my right, Sen. Francis Pangilinan. Elsewhere was Sen. Risa Hontiveros. Fr. Reyes's sermonette was somewhat political, not inappropriately, given the zeitgeist. So was

Bobby's. Mass over. CJ Meilou arrived with hubby. She took the seat vacated by Raul, to my left; he had departed with fellow Liberal Kiko, right after the Mass.

Juan Perez III, MD, aka Doc Jeepy, made the opening remarks and Ms. Myrna (Meth, hmmm) Jimenez, the closing. Both are Bantayog's Trustees. Millennial Ralyn Rodriguez, PUP Students Party Chairman and President of Central Student Council also spoke. Bobby spoke too. Aba, provocateur din pala gaya ni Father Reyes.

Then Ka Oca Santos, 89, whose magnificent obsession is for the farmers to get their share of the coconut levy fund in the billions. He is a fellow son of Quezon. A Maubanin, I was among those who spoke. I said a benefit of martial law was I got to know and get close to the likes of Ka Tanny and Ka Pepe. Watching them handle a case was like looking over the shoulders of Picasso and Rembrandt, while painting.

We were given flowers to strew. To conclude, we fervently sang Bayan Ko, and the CJ, singing, also had her right arm up thrust in the air, the human rights salute (I earlier remarked that I just saw again Digong doing the Nazi salute of right arm thrust forward, fist clenched, a criminal act in countries Hitler subjugated and terrorized.)

Cookie Diokno also spoke along with Atty. Petong Sawali, Sen. Leila's chief of staff.

I mentioned my recollection of an account of how Tanny's Ermat had to discipline him as a machito teen in Gumaca, Quezon with four GFs! Simul, not a Serial Lady Killer. Later, he, along with Ka Pepe, Uncle Jovy S, et al. were paradigmatic prayerful padres de familia. (I do have questions as to Bobby T, nagtitina pa, hmmm, in his second adolescence din yata. Pare, ingat, nandyan si Zeny, baka magaya ka kay Tsikboy Joe Calida; scuttlebut is na-Elin Nordegren-treatment , like Tiger Woods. 9-Ironed. Araguy.)

MABINI clients Doris Baffrey and Jovy Labajo, of the April 6 Liberation Movement, were there. So were Paco Alcuaz, Mon Casiple, Ed Garcia, Pete Lacaba, Noel Medina, the Nemenzos, Joel Paredes, Etta Rosales, Salonga apos, Isagani Serrano, and many many other veterans of the Struggle. But, so were the millennials, in numbers.

I began by saying that the night before I had to forego ballroom dancexercising, a Saturday staple, to make sure I'd get up early for Tanny, for whom I'd go to the ends of the earth.

Gone Ka Tanny was on May 28, 1992 and indeed, when a great tree falls, one sees how barren the landscape is.

Ceres Doyo and Jo Ann Maglipon were there too and said MABINI stalwart Jun Factoran was in some hospital to go under the knife. Prayers. Latest bulletin: Successful operation but no visitors allowed at this time. I rightly dunno why Tsikboy JunFac reminds me of how Ka Tanny was in his youth. No whiff of any scandal marred the record of Ka Tanny. And JunFac, take heart, di lang tayo Attys., MDs pa, Masasamang Damo.

Excerpts from my talk: I opened thusly "At my back is the picture of Ka Tanny making the human rights salute after his 1978 arrest. Prez

Digong makes his guests do the Nazi salute with arms thrust forward with clenched fist, criminal in places in Europe Hitler trodded on decades ago. Aussie Spymaster Nick Warner did it with Digong last year and he got hammered, pummelled and pilloried from pillar to post.

"I had heard of Ka Tanny in my youth but I had no yen for politics. The first time I met him was in September 1967 when we bumped into each other in crowded Harvard Square. He was there for Harvard Law's sesquicentennial.

"When martial law was inflicted, one of its blessings was I got to know close-up inspiring patriots I otherwise might not have met, like Ka Tanny. So thank you, Mr. Marcos. We gravitated to people like Ka Tanny, whose uncompromising code from the start was Resist!Resist! Resist!

"Then the 1978 LABAN episode; as campaign general manager he led us in what he called a `mad adventure.&# 39; We'd meet in his office where, once Ka Pepe and Joker Arroyo arrived, Ka Tanny would lock the door, pull out a bottle, to start Happy Hour with the two. I am a teetotaler. No alak for me.

"In 1978, after we in Laban were cheated the opposition planned to demo in front of the Manila Cathedral, where we would rendezvous. The group of Ka Tanny, Joker, Soc Rodrigo and his sons, Tito and Ruth Guingona, Ernie Rondon, et al., marching, from QC, was stopped; they were arrested. Ka Tanny's pix with fist thrust upwards remains vivid in my mind. Now we have the Nazi salute of Digong, with clenched fist thrust forward, a criminal act elsewhere.

"When we founded MABINI in 1980, he generously agreed to be our Honorary Chair.

"Fast forward to September 1984. Pixes there are of our group at the Welcome Rotunda. Attacked with water hoses and truncheons, we stood our ground (with my foolish heart, I even charged! Talagang sira). Ka Tanny, 86, and Bobby, were drenched, along with Lean Alejandro, Frank Chavez, Inday Nita Daluz, Fr. Joe Dizon, Tito Guingona, Ed Garcia, Nonoy Sarabia, Lorna Verano-Yap, et al..

"I cannot now recall when last Ka Tanny and I met. But, what won't ever be beyond easy recall was his gesture on September 16, 1991 when the Senate voted to end our status as America' s Last Plantation. After Uncle Jovy announced, `the treaty is defeated,' Ka Tanny arose from his wheelchair and thrust his clenched fist upward.

"To quote from Thomas Gray, in his Elegy in a Country Churchyard, Ka Tanny was a `gem of purest ray serene.'

"Millennials and adolescents of all ages, I am reminded of an anecdote about a mischievous boy who planned to put one over on the old wise man in the mountain. With a pipit at his back, and thinking that depending on Lolo's answer, he would either release or crush it, he confidently thought that no matter what, mali si Lolo. "Pag sinabing patay, palalayin ko lang, pag buhay, pipisain ko lang, kahit anong sagot nita, tiyak mali. Tiklo siya'

"Lolo, good morning po, ito ho bang pipit sa likod ko, patay o buhay?"

"Nagisip sandali si Lolo at sumagot, `anak, ang kasasagutan ay nasa iyong mga kamay,'

"So my young friends, the millennials, as our shadows lengthen - in the last quarter, or two minutes, or in the pre-departure area, the answer is in your hands.

"Thank you for making it possible to share some of my thoughts and concerns with you, and may I blame those concerned, for making it necessary.

Was it necessary to insult Compañero Philip Jurado in firing him? "You SOB, you are fired!" It seems to me civility is needed in the civil service. If high officials do not get due process, wh**o will**? DECAY seems to be truly here. A son, I gather, of iconic Desi Jurado, a true Bessang Pass hero, Philip deserves better in this Fire!Aim!Ready! administration. "Hit me, but hear me first" - an ancient cry.

In the wage increase trilemma, who speaks for the unorganized eleven million jobless? Indeed, who asks foolish questions about Boracay being land-reformed?

Saguisag & Associates Lawyers 4045 Bigasan Street, Palanan 1235 Makati Office Nos. (+632) 551-6350/833- 4140 Fax No. (+632) 831-2276

Oooooo

8

IMPEACHMENT SUPERIOR; REMEMBERING ED ANGARA

May 17, 2018

Early last month, Prez Duterte described Chief (CJ) Justice Sereno as his "enemy, to be outed", or words to that effect. That arguably sealed her fate, which began when she took exception to his naming and shaming judges without due process. Those concerned I perceive and liken to the four knights who had heard Henry II ask: "Who will rid me of this boisterous priest?" They considered themselves told. And the fate of Archbishop Thomas Becket was sealed.

She lost 8-6 (I assume all the Justices who voted were physically present, as is required elsewhere such as in Congress; absentee voting should not do as a last-minute debate, appeal or argument in the continuing cross-fertilization of ideas may carry the day).

From the moment Digong proclaimed her his "enemy, " what was predictable followed. What did not was the very close voting (Rep. Rey Umali had predicted, 11-3; bulaang propeta.) Unanimity was the factor that made it easy for the U.S. Supreme Court to have its rulings accepted in controversial, emotionally- charged cases. Examples range from Brown v. Board of Education of Topeka, 418 U.S. 683 (1954) outlawing racial segregation, or U.S. v. Nixon, 418 U.S. 683 (1974), ordering Nixon surrender the Watergate tapes. All the way to denying Clinton' s plea for postponement of his impeachment trial. Clinton v. Jones, 520 U.S. 681 (1997). Not a single dissent. And the nation moved on.

8-6 was as close as it could be (Meilou showed more class in recusing herself than those perceived publicly to have an animus towards her. In my view, they should also have inhibited themselves, but chose not to, revolutionizing our jurisprudence on recusation, where mere perception ranked high, even if not well-grounded (para wala na lang pong masabi) - the Caesar's wife test of being above suspicion.

If quo warranto (QW) had come ahead of impeachment, maybe the Justices concerned would not have gone to the House to broadcast their animosity, and the people and history would presume good faith. It took Cong. Vicente Veloso (former Court of Appeals Justice) to raise the use of QW, per media reports.

As a policy matter, removing a peer should not be left to the unelected Supreme Court Justices, with their conceivable personal biases and grievances. It is said that men think they are thinking when in fact they are merely rearranging their prejudices - William James. That is why the need for judicial restraint, to protect one from himself, so that the PEOPLE, thru their ELECTED Congressmen and Senators, can decide the fate of impeachable officials; the voting would be far easier to sell than what a few UNELECTED alone decide. Impeachment is political after all, not judicial.

A less restrictive alternative, far superior to QW, a road not earlier taken, leading as it would seem, to a precipice.

When the Constitution speaks of removal through impeachment, it excludes other modes. Expressio unius est exclusio alterius.

The Senate should assert its prerogative and duty, and not watched idly while a loved one is being violated in the violet time in the vilest possible way.

But, indeed, great cases, like hard cases, make bad law - Holmes.

The 8-6 ruling might or should land on the wrong side of history like the unlamented Javellana v. Executive Secretary decision of March 31, 1973 on the scandalous 6-4 "ratification& quot; of the 1973 Constitution in Barangay Assemblies. The attendees were asked "sino sa inyo ang may gusto ng siopao?" The raised hands were counted as "yes," per the account of 1986 Constitutional Commissioner Pepe Nolledo, a patriot of the first water.

So was his fellow Con-Con Delegate Edong Angara, who left us last Sunday. Ed voted to convict a Chief Justice in 2012. How I wish the foolish story that he, Manong Johnny Ponce Enrile and 18 others had been bribed with pork would now stop.

Who will land on the right side of history here? Ed definitely will and what follows was what I said in gist in eulogy the other day in the Senate.

"To all my golden friends gathered here this morning to bid goodbye to one we honor, today - and always will - in his final sentimental journey home, a home of which he was the patriarch, for many a year - good morning.

"These last few days I lost two, both from Quezon, the first being my eldest brother, Tony, Jr., born in 1937 in Mauban (birthplace of Fr. Horacio de la Costa and Ninez Cacho Olivares), and the other, Edong, born in Baler in 1934, my `spiritual brother,' a term he used in emailing me on June 16, 2015.

"A kinder Kuya than quiet engineer Junior I could not have found and a better public servant and statesman, than soft-spoken Compañero Edong one cannot find easily, either.

"His biography, In the Grand Manner, was launched in late April, 2015. He was quoted at the time as having said that his life had been `far from perfect.' Characteristically self-deprecating. But, it was a life well-lived indeed, as many say. (And the only perfect lawyer I know anyway was a fellow Bedan, Justice Gregorio Perfecto, Clase Superior, 1905. But for high school, "my first choice was San Beda," Ed wrote in his bio, at page 10.)

"Last we met was last March 23, during the launch of the Fulbright Hall of Fame. The first was in the 1971-72 ConCon in Manila Hotel, where I was my Pasig townsman Delegate Bobbit Sanchez' s go-fer. Ed had asked another townsman, Aveling Cruz, bar No. 1 at 20, and ACCRA co-founder, to set up lunch with Ed in that venue. Ed asked me ever so gently to consider co-founding ACCRA. But, by then I had founded the San Beda Free Legal Aid Clinic and was set to become what would later be known as a human rights lawyer, an animal unknown when I was in law schools, here and abroad. [In the June 16, 2015 email, he reminded me, "had you agreed to join us, you would have been a founding partner of ACCRALAW. . . . You said you would study the offer and later you declined my invitation. [The same way I declined a signed Supreme Court appointment in late January, 1987. My sanity continues to be questioned, jury still out.]

"Ed and I, both less than perfect in an uncertain world, had our differences then on martial law which lasted long but, where I was perhaps tactless and unkind he was ever so tactful and tolerant, like a forgiving Kuya.

"A turning point from where I sat was his NAMFREL role in the 1985-86 snap elections, a game for all the marbles, the whole enchilada. He, like Manang Letty Ramos-Shahani, distanced himself from the dictator when it was risky to do so. Electrifying. In times of moral crises, one cannot be neutral, per Dante. "(BTW, my co-Rizal Hi alum Cora de la Paz Bernardo, was also active in NAMFREL, and was also recognized last March 23 as a Pioneer Fulbrighter.)"

"Ed was among Prez Cory's 1987 choices; more than impressed, she picked him as a Senate bet and he was decisively voted into office by an appreciative, grateful, discerning people."

"Long before his autobiography was launched, we had become fast friends, with a deep and abiding respect for each other's, at times, differing views on what was best for the Motherland.

"I am reminded of what Wordsworth wrote, `what though the radiance which was once so bright, be now forever taken from [our] sight, though nothing can bring back the hour, of splendor in the grass, of glory in the flower, grieve not, rather find, strength in what remains behind [and] in years that bring a philosophic mind'.

"Ed, we thank you, we salute you as we find strength in what you leave behind."

"Goodbye and Godspeed - to your deeply-deserved eternal reward."

"It was joyous if solemn affair to celebrate the life and times of a great Filipino patriot (but the dignity was to me sort of marred only when a Senator to my right and a Senator to my left who will remain mercifully unnamed - showed me their CPs disclosing that the Boston Celtics had just again beaten the Cleveland Cavaliers in the ongoing NBA playoffs. The Celts were my late wife's fave, having spent two years in Boston College for her Master's in social work, on a full scholarship. Senator Sonny Angara said in his response that Ed's parents did not have to spend for his tuition and free public education was one many splendored dream Ed had worked hard for. Now a reality."

Again, TY, Ed, for everything you have done, to give the Filipino a chance - for a better life. For us, "the work goes on, the cause endures, the hope still lives, and the dream [for a better life}, shall never die."

oooooo

9

'SURTOUT, PAS TROP DE ZELE' – TALLEYRAND

May 10, 2018

It must have been in 1969 when I read Dean Acheson' s Present at the Creation. That was how I was introduced to Talleyrand's advice to diplomats which, that book said, meant "above all, no zeal." Elliptical it was, I now see.

Given the lack of zeal and how pussycat-pusillanim ous the administration seems towards irrendentist China in the West Philippine Sea dispute, it may be hard to see our President as a Strong Man, as otherwise correctly described named by TIME (in its May 14, 2018 issue where he shares the cover with Putin and two others). He seems to be always asking China, "what else can we do for you, Master?" Let us see what he will say and do when he visits Philippine Rise. Surpise us, Sir.

He now says China is protecting us.(?) From itself? Or as its 24th province?*

Given the pixes of military hardware supposedly being erected by China, is the supposed Strongman not a marshmallow in reality in the West Philippine Sea context? He blames the U.S., which he keeps insulting, and "softie" PNoy, who had the good fortune of serendipitously retaining my pal, Paul Reichler, a veteran Harvard Law transnational warrior, in the arbitral case, and won; however, Digong, said and seen to be a brawler, minimized and put it in the back burner.

The Palace mouthpiece said it would check the veracity of the militarization reports. Still checking? Last February, Digong dismissively said the missiles were not aimed at us anyway. But, the checking was supposed to have started a year ago. The administration must use a faster banca, as jetski seems to be out, along with Tora Toras. (One such jurassic aircraft was used in a coup against Prez Cory, to bomb Camp Crame, and nearly hit Nene Pimentel in his Marikina home, it was said.) Will the Prez really go next week and tell the Chinese where to go?

Next month, Prez Digong will have been in power for two years, when the build-up intensified, opportunist China seeing how he adores its leader, not one to miss an opportunity. (Again, it was Talleyrand who said a woman may forgive a man who forces an opportunity, but never a man who misses one.) No zeal in warding off China, whose citizens are gobbling up real property in our country. Are they a potential Fifth Column supporting four other columns as General Vidal saw in the Spanish Civil War? My late Mommy told me about Japanese boarders in Lola's Mauban, Tayabas (now Quezon) home who turned out to be advance troopers when the invasion came.

And will we have our treacherous Vidkun Quislings?

Zeal we seemed to have too much of, in Kuwait. Our foreign affairs people should not have forgotten French Foreign Minister Talleyrand's complete classic epigram: "Above all, not too much zeal." An evergreen dictum going back two centuries. (The Talleyrand I fantasize, also said he would prefer an army of 100 sheep led by a lion - a red one, from San Beda - to a hundred lions led by a sheep.)

Also going back two centuries, last October 26-29, Harvard Law marked its 200th anniversary. Per a bulletin I got on the event last week, "[i]t was a joyous weekend filled with laughter, friendship and a lot of dancing." Were my late Dulce still around, may I also daydream, we might have gone and danced up a storm, doing the jive/boogie with an endless spin, round-and-round, which I still try to do today. But, the old fire and energy are gone, with but a few smoldering sparks remaining.

Anyhow, I teach Saturdays. Our Rizal High School class'55 meets every quarter but only during Saturdays (so I had been a no-show in the quarterly reunions all these years). Conflicting classes in Mendiola and Alabang.

Last Saturday though, I met my Mendiola class briefly to enable me to meet with high school chums in Ado's Panciteria in Malinao, Pasig, for the first time, ever, for lunch. I had thought it was time to heed Mark Twain and Walter Hagen, who wrote, not to hurry, not to worry, we're here only for a short visit, so why not stop and smell the flowers along the way? It was joyous, filled with laughter, friendship and a little dancing - a cha cha exhibition by one of the dolls. In the end, I helped lead the class in fervently singing auld lang syne. Indeed, the friends of one's youth are priceless, per Robert Penn Warren. Other ballads like Little Things Mean a Lot we sang with feeling.

On the ballad of 16th Justice Jomar Canlas, who covers mostly seniors in Padre Faura, his initiative and enterprise enable him to scoop all others on how a Supreme Court decision would go. Hangga ngayon di po mapupulaang siya'y isang bulaang propeta.

Leaks discourage full-blown robust and uninhibited discussion lest a devil advocate' s position be misrepresented as a Justice' s opinion. Unless we return to the leak-proof judiciary of old, we will continue to decay. Retired Justice Bobby Abad reportedly said for the Supreme Court to close shop if those concerned would continue to talk, unethically, about exchanges in closed-door executive sessions. Yet, no move to probe we hear.

I remember how in one case I handled as a private prosecutor before Manila CFI Judge Jose Alejandro, only at the hour of promulgation did he read the dispositive portion handwritten at dawn, acquitting or convicting. That was how our respected courts treated confidential material before martial law inaugurated our rot and decay, which arguably continue today, from where I sit. We worshipped the gods in Mt. Olympus then and had the highest regard for very professional court personnel, who just helped in deciding cases (not in demo-ing. for crying out loud).

In the Harvard Bulletin mentioned above, shown were a majority of the U.S. Supreme Court, Harvard Law alums all, led by John Roberts,'79 arguably an outsider who was named

Chief Justice at 50, without provoking any static or discontent. The others were J. David Souter,'66, Elena Kagan,'86, J. Stephen G. Breyer,'64, Anthony M. Kennedy,'61, and Neil Gorsuch,'91.

All of them know that as Justices, they have in Washington, D.C.. one role to play: to decide cases. Thus, the clean, not clogged, dockets. Above all, not too much zeal and ambition. Just plain hard toil with their Chief so named in 2005, who's only 63 today. There is no talk of removing one so young, much younger when first appointed.

Last month, on removing our young Chief Justice, I wrote that in the Solicitor General' s Quo Warranto petition, he unexpectedly hammered on R.A. No. 3019, thusly: "80. . . . As early as 1960, Congress imposed that requirement in R.A. No. 3019. Section 7 of the law [says that] . . . Every public officer . . . shall prepare and file a true detailed and sworn statement of assets and liabilities, including a statement of the amounts and sources of his income, the amounts of his personal and family expenses and the amount of income taxes paid for the next preceding calendar year: .. ."

I then said if the SolGen can show me a copy of a statement timely filed by any incumbent where he stated his income, expenses and taxes, I'll eat it. I now have a copy of his latest filing, which I don't have to eat. He has not reported his income, expenses and taxes, either, as required by law.

Noncompliance with what he requires is massive and will mean the impeachment of all impeachable officials and the removal of the rest. The policy consideration or solution in our scofflaw society is to amnesty the massive violation with a warning of severity in the coming year. The SolGen should not be zealous in implementing the law, fair on its face, with an evil eye and an uneven hand - J. Matthews.*

oooooo

10

ARROGANCE OF POWER; TAUNTING AND GAMESMANSHIP

May 2, 2018

On our relationship with Kuwait, no one knows what may happen next, but the cosmic roll of the dice will in time tell, as it were. If we are able to spirit away someone abroad, in inhumane condition, quietly, unadvertised, no braggadocio, kudos.

But, rubbing it in is another matter, via videotape even gone viral - of the flagrant violation of sovereignty.

We cannot tell Kuwait where to go, if only because many of our countrymen go there, to work and support their cash-strapped families left behind. Now, they are told to go home - and risk starvation.

In the National Basketball Association (NBA), one who makes a powerful dunk may slightly brag but taunting could be assessed a technical. No need to provoke childishly. "It' s their playground. They are the home team. We play by their rules, or blow the ball game." (Sidney Sheldon in Windmills of the Gods.)

A player who thumps his chest and yell like Tarzan should not do it in front of the fans and players of the host arena. He may risk being lynched, as it were.

We may have to play the game in Kuwait by their rules, not ours, as Marcos and Duterte have egregiously shown, but here; Kuwait is not one of our backwater resorts or provinces. It is sovereign.

Quiet gamesmanship may be understandable but to taunt and brag by circulating a video on how we trampled on another' s sovereignty is a tactless No-No.

I remember an NBA game where a Philly Six'er (Billy Cunningham, if my fading memory is true) was shown decades ago on instant replay, as ever so gently nudging an opponent out of the way and getting the ball. Not seen by the refs, chalk it to smart gamesmanship. But, if the congenial Kangaroo Kid Hall of Famer Billy had romped across the court and bragged about the feat, by beating his chest and bellowing, a la Tarzan, technical foul, at the least.

Here, we may have committed a technical foul in international law. Indeed, some excitable Pinoys have in effect childishly dirty-fingered Kuwait. Totally unnecessary, this show of childishness.

Imagine if another country would have done here what we have done in Kuwait, spirit out an abused alien. For lack of faith in the locals, strong diplomatic protest, except maybe if the culprit were China which has been doing far worse things, from where I sit, in the disputed maritime area, than we have done in Kuwait. Missiles installed in the West Philippine Sea? Never mind, says the Palace, they are not aimed at us anyway but at the U.S. (where millions of Filipinos, like Loida Nicolas-Lewis, and other decent patriotic people, live).

Kuwaitis, we may quietly badmouth here but we don't taunt them in their own arena, or internationally, even.

In Latin America, they went to war over soccer football (balonpie). In the 100-hour Football War between El Salvador and Honduras in 1969, thousands of lives were lost. The causes were far more complex than balonpie of course but the simplest unintended consequence is the poor became poorer.

May we wish President Dutere bon voyage as he sails to Philippine Rise any day now and assert ownership. He vows to go to war over it and there's always the risk of winning of course, as Vietnam has shown in defeating France and the United States. PUSO or HEART Vietnam showed in blocking China's incursion in 1979, with 30,000 lives lost. China retreated.

Has Didong retreated on ENDO? If ending ENDO is legislated by executive order, good for the employed, but, what about the unemployed (now close to 11,000,000)? I was once in the commanding heights of Malacañang myself, in

1986, and had a panoramic view. At times, our choices would be 1) bad, 2) worse and 3) worst, and so no matter how we decided, there would be carping, taunting and heckling, from the bivouacs.

No pleasing everyone when in government.

So, what do the hungry in Boracay want? Or those who may come home from Kuwait? Again, the rescue may have been admirable derring do, gamesmanship, maybe in violation of Kuwait's sovereignty. But, was it necessary to rub it in and advertise and circulate the humiliation? Time and again, we see it being done locally, but in another country, we need more tact. Just because we can get away with arrogance of power here does not mean it can have extraterritorial reach without unnecessary and undesirable complications.

We see such arrogance in deporting Sister Patricia Fox, in not factoring in the welfare of the Boracay residents, in removing the Comfort Women statue, in entertaining quo warranto filed way out of time, etc...

Our nearly eleven million jobless may be invited to a Barmecidal feast. The EJKs have not reduced them enough. Arabian Prince Barmecide invited a beggar to a fictional banquet but if one reads through to the end of the enchanting fairy tale, the game of Pretend did have a happy ending. Ojala! as they may say in Spain and Kuwait.

Back home in Mendiola, young high school organ staffers writing critically of our most well-known and powerful alum, had their work censored, I was given to understand. But, again, as family, we must survive our crises, mend the ruptures of our discord and continue to live and function as a unit.

To be president, according to Jack Kennedy, he had dreamnt, because - the presidency is where the power is. Agreed, but surely the powerful can abide dissent out of prudential considerations. Oh, how many crimes have been committed by the administration through reckless imprudence, as malice is not to be presumed. Generally. Abangan.

Finally, I would not tell the Kuwaitis to go to hell. They may come here, recalling what Quezon said about a Philippines run by our very own for decades now.

Saguisag & Associates Lawyers 4045 Bigasan Street, Palanan1235 Makati Office Nos. (+632) 551-6350/833- 4140Fax No. (+632) 831-2276*

oooooo

11

ZUGZWANG? OR SWISCHZENZUG?

Apr 25, 2018

Last Monday, Sandiganbayan Justice Bernie Fernandez made his final sentimental journey home (San Beda, Home of Quality Products, a term Justice Florenz Regalado would borrow from San Miguel, in the 60's).Bernie was

No.. 5 in the 1954 bar exams, Flor, No. 1 the following year, with 96.7% a record-breaking mark that may stand until the desert sands grow cold (as in Boracay, at noon). Bernie's son, Lito, is now a Sandiganbayan Justice himself, validating that fruit does not fall or roll far from the tree.

I first heard of Bernie's" home-going" by text. Last Monday, another text came, saying that Manang Leticia Aquino, mother of San Beda Graduate School of Law Dean Father Rannie was also gone. Our prayers.. Fr. Rannie is one of the eloquent voices on many issues from Mendiola, which does not speak with a single voice in contributing to the sounds and noises of democracy. (Not heard last Monday was Law Dean Gil Jara, who had to leave the Abbey Church because of a dizzy spell partly traceable to the very hot weather we are having.) So, what's this I hear that our high school studes are barred from criticizing the administration?

Our editorial last Sunday said Chief Justice (CJ) Meilou Sereno may now be inzugzwang, a German term for a situation where a chessplayer has no good move ina losing, delicate situation. If the polls are to be believed, the public is disappointed by the squabbling Supreme Court (SC). I have to question whether only she is to blame, if at all. Is the entire judiciary in zugzwang? I think everyone in the SC who detours from his or her primordial duty to decide cases and prefers in-house dogfights and catfights is a cause of the dip in rating. Along with the shocking leaks to Justices Jomar Canlas and Mon Tulfo which have yet to trigger an internal probe by the seemingly unconcerned magistrates (who really should not judge their own cause). Retired Justice Bobby Abad reportedly once said the SC might as well close shop if confidentiality is not restored and preserved. Has any Justice asked for or initiated a probe toregain public confidence, by 1) stopping leaks (no contempt this time) and 2) aborting revolutionizing the rules on recusation?

Onthe Kenquoy Warranto, Sec. 7 of R.A. No. 3019 on reporting one's sources and amounts of income, personal and family expenses and taxes paid is violated by the Prez (I have a copy of his noncompliant 2017 filing). Indeed, I believe noncompliant himself is the SolGen himself, along with everyone else in government. Else, some student of mine would have shown proof of compliance, by someone, somewhere, after all these years. The lapse is not impeachable, else all impeachable officials should now also be impeached (and others removed otherwise); non-compliance, in my view, does not rise to the level of an impeachable offense, one so serious and enormous as to affect the very core and workings of government. So, with all due respect, the CJ is not in zugzwang, unless we mean the entire SC is. What we have may be a swischzenzug, more like Bobby Fischer' s 19RB6! – against Pal Benko in the 1963 U.S. Chess championships. A quiet intermediate move before the Killer Shot. Who made the move - Meilou or the arguably Biased Five, through the SolGen? The bigger pix we have to look at. We may yet have a changed judiciary, leak-proof, as before, after the lessons that would have been learned in the impeachment and Kenquoy warranto complaints lodged against the CJ. Truelove of country is needed. *Non sibi sed patriae*. Not self but country. Expressed in various ways respectful of the culture concerned. Here, Veep Leni Robredo & Co. got hammered for taking souvenirs shots in the Berlin Holocaust Memorial. The uproar from the anti-Leni camp sounded like the possible understandable reaction had she and her group made the Nazi salute with rights arms thrust forward, a criminal act that could have led to the group being prosecuted. Or the Gadon "You're No.1" gesture with the middle finger. But, not mere Kodakan, for crying out loud! Having a pix among one's souvenirs is most natural and understandable. No word from the powerful and alert ubiquitous Anti-Jewish Defamation League. Leni and her party had nothing to apologize for. Absolutely. (Digong reportedly apologized to Kuwait - way to go.)

Aside from the predictable local usual suspects, I have yet to hear from any Jewish source, a most vilified and persecuted but militant minority, bitching. They fight disrespect, not harmless innocent pix-taking. What could be more natural than taking a souvenir photo say in Rizal Monument in Luneta, Lincoln Memorial, Libingan ng Mga Bayani (Atbp.), Fort Bonifacio American Cemetery, the Verdun -They Shall Not Pass - Museum, the Les Invalides in Paris or in Valle de los Caidos (Valley of the Fallen, which has a Benedictine Abbey in the complex)? The latter reminds me of the Siege of the Alcazar where, in the 1936 Spanish Civil War, Col.

Moscardo Ituarte, on July 23, was put on the line with Luio, his16-year-old son, who said "Father, I was arrested this morning, if you won't surrender in ten minutes, they will execute me." Said the father," In that case, commend yourself to the Lord, cry Via El Cristo Rey! Cry Viva Espana!, and die like a hero." Luis replied, "That I'll do, Father. Goodbye." He was shot to death immediately thereafter. Father and son did not whine like Bato de la Rosa na masakit 'yun.

The women in the Fort, forbidden to cook and help nurse wounds, for their safety, offered safe-conduct by the aggressors, refused and said if need be, they themselves would fight, boosting the defenders' already high morale. Today, the telephone remains in the Fort, a reminder of Spanish honor, nobility, militancy, bravery and patriotism. It should make for a nice souvenir picture backdrop, with no one to complain of disrespect.

The Siege of the Alcazar was staged in San Beda at least a decade before Digong enrolled there, where we were earlier taught, "Lo cortes no quita lovaliente" - courtesy does not detract from valor.. Now PI! is what we hear from our fellow alum from San Beda, now in a tight fix of sorts because of the positions Ateneo and La Salle have vocally taken on Meilou's perceived Zugzwang. Not to mention the roaring Bedan high school studes.

Non sibi sed patriae, not self but country, is apparently not in the vocabulary or consciousness of the huge Duterte forces. The entire judiciary may be seen to be falling. Let's hope the supposed zugzwang is in fact a swiszchenzug leading to internal reform such as plugging leaks, for starters, or else close shop, according to respected retired Justice Bobby Abad.

Today, we have rumors of which certain retiring Justices would be rewarded with new appointments. Should that happen, tuloy tuloy na po tayo sa pagbulusok sa balon ng kapariwaraan. The SC may never recover as Digong takes total control of all branches. From his commanding heights, he ordered Sister Patricia Fox detained, usurping what only trial judges can authorize after some preliminary determination where an accused is heard. And home Down Under she is bound for.(?)

No due process. No court or agency would dare embarrass him. Hitler also took absolute power totally in accord with constitutional processes as the ramparts fell with hardly any struggle, according to Lon Luvois Fuller. But, Hitler is not now remembered for the People' s Car (Volkswagen or Beetle). Mussolini is not remembered for making the trains run on time, either.

The CJ will be remembered for standing at the last rampart and may go down in flames for judicial independence. A Queen Sacrifice in chess.(?) How will the other Justices land in history? Like the Marcosian magistrates?

Do they wonder whose small plane Duterte used in flying to and from Singapore? He is not allowed to accept gifts. How many of his security, medical team and support staff had to fly separately to and from by commercial aircraft? Who would dare question the presidential practice or gesture in some court for illegality and impropriety? The sky is falling.(?)

oooooo

12

The ICC, Ka Pepe and Human Rights

Apr 4, 2018

Today marks the ruby anniversary of the memorable April 6, 1978 Noise Barrage after which the April 6 Liberation Movement was named. The intrepid Movement , client of MABINI, was necessary, but not sufficient, to stop the gross human rights violations then going on.

No sovereign country strictly needs the International Criminal Court (ICC) but its poor obscure powerless inhabitants may. To withdraw from it may be another manifestation of a world in decay, a big step in the wrong direction.. During martial law, we needed Prez Jimmy Carter, Senator John Kerry, State Asec Pat Derian, et al., and Amnesty International to alleviate the plight of Marcosian human rights victims. We were more grateful than we could say for their "meddling"; in the spirit of the Universal Declaration of Human Rights our country had helped forge.

During Holy Week last, virtually no attention was given by media to the pioneer Hall-of-Famers in the Fulbright Philippines 70th Anniversary Gala Dinner - Reflections on 70 years of Excellence night, at Manila Pen. The trailblazers were Angel C. Alcala, Bienvenido L. Lumbera, Bienvenido F. Nebres, SJ, Clare R. Baltazar, Napoleon V. Abueva, Abdulmari Asia Imao, Lucrecia R. Casilag and Conchita M. Abad, in the order their names appeared in the program. Joey Cuisia was No. 2, Cora de la Paz-Bernardo was No. 3 and I was No. 6. Thanks to Fulbright, I got to roam in the sacred precincts of Harvard Yard and in its law school in 1967-68.

During the dark years, students there got to read about the great Filipino Senator-Lawyer from Batangas, whose 31st death anniversary we marked last February 27, thusly: "It is pertinent to recall the wise words of Jose Diokno in rejecting what he termed `currently fashionable justifications for authoritarianism in Asian developing countries.&# 39; One [justification] is that Asian societies are authoritarian and paternalistic; that Asia's hungry masses are too concerned with providing their families with food, clothing, and shelter, to concern themselves with civil liberties and political freedoms; that the Asian conception of freedom differs from that of the West; that, in short, Asians are not fit for human rights.

[This] is racist nonsense . . . . Authoritarianism promotes repression not development - repression that prevents meaningful change and preserves the structures of power and privilege. . . ." H. Steiner & D. Vagst, Transnational Legal Transactions 445-46 (1986)..

The two authors were excellent team-teachers and I was lucky to have both. I am checking whether the quoted passage is carried in later editions. How we have fallen in the world's esteem since 1986. We may fall even deeper now in that too many people have died since Digong won, and he is now petulantly trying to withdraw from the ICC. Justice Claro M. Recto used the term "human rights" in 1936; that, from where I sit, was the first recorded use of the term in local jurisprudence. He is very much a part of our tradition in the great lawyer interpretation of history. In an easement case, he said: "The evidence discloses that this passage-way across the Hacienda `Begoña' is the same one frequented by carabaos . . . . Plaintiff intends not only to prohibit the defendants from using the road in question, but also from crossing the lands of the Hacienda 'Begoña,&# 39; also belonging to the plaintiff, where carabaos are allowed to roam. An act so shocking to the conscience, one is reminded, could only have been perpetrated during the feudal period when human rights were unmercifully sacrificed to property rights." North Negros Sugar Co. v. Hidalgo, 63 Phil. 664, 6.

We should arrest decay and feudalistic atavism and stay in the ICC. In another human rights area, who speaks for the young children victimized in divorce? Or those still in the womb? No one in the Cabinet, in the House nor in the Senate speaks for them. Who speaks for the commuter who will miss Uber? Judge Learned Hand counselled that "[m]any people believe that possession of unchallenged economic power deadens initiative, discourages thrift and depresses energy; that immunity from competition is a narcotic, and rivalry is a stimulant to economic progress; that the spur of constant stress is necessary to counteract an inevitable disposition to let well enough alone." United States v. Aluminum Co. of America, 148 F.2d 416, 427 (2d Cir. 1945). But Grab may grouse that monopoly was thrust upon it by market forces.

More disturbing is the sorry attempt to silence all competition and opposition, jailing Senator Leila de Lima, impeaching and Kenquoy-Warrantoing Chief Justice Meilou Sereno, ostracizing Rappler, Sonny Trillanes, et al., which could lead to a functional equivalent of a Jacksonian unanimity of the graveyard.

In the Kenquoy Warranto case, the SolGen saps CJ Meilou for not reporting income earned, expenses incurred, and taxes paid, required by Sec. 7 of R.A. No. 3019, the Tolentino anti-graft law of 1960.

May I repeat my challenge, if the Solgen can show me compliance by him, by any of his 17 assistants who signed the Kenquoy Warranto petition, or by any sitting or retired justice, I'll eat it. Certainly, it cannot be an impeachable offense,

if only given the massive noncompliance with a law more honored in the breach than in the observance. Not enough jails to house all violators.

All these many years, I have kept asking my studes to produce proof of compliance with Sec. 7 of R.A. No. 3019 (not Sec. 8 of R.A. No. 6713), by anyone among the million and a half in the Civil Service - in vain.

Can anyone in the supernumerary Presidential Anti-Crime Commish show his compliance with Sec. 7 of R.A. No. 3019? (And I have my doubt as to whether the Prez could create such an office, the task really of our pusillanimous meow-meow or bow-wow-wow Congress, with its obsolescent power of the purse.)

To hold the CJ liable under the SolGen's theory is to find oneself liable.

And I maintain that any Justice who has openly shown animosity to CJ Sereno cannot sit in judgment in her case, egregiously failing the Caesr's wife test in inhibition or recusation, routinely and repeatedly counselled by the Supreme Court.

"Above suspicion " is the operative term, to maintain the Rule of Law. Unaware that a quo warranto petition would be lodged, certain innocent Justices have talked too much and the only honorable course to take now is to recuse themselves, that CJ Meilou may have a sporting chance. They cannot judge their own cause. Credibility and legitimacy matter. They answer to their conscience and to history.

Let the impeachment trial go through. The sub judice rule of silence should apply to the Senators-Judges, used to mischievous play-by-play announcement long before all the evidence is in, but not to the public, in this political exercise, not litigation with its accepted limitation that no one observes hereabouts anyway. No premature ejac seen in Fire!Ready!Aim! congressional hearings.

And the Supreme Court leaks like a sieve. You wanna know what the SC will do? Subscribe to the best paper in town and read enterprising 16th Justice Jomar Canlas. Talaga pong hindi bulaang propeta. His mobility in the SC's sacred precincts is legendary.

A leaky SC inhibits and stifles free and robust discussion and the taksil leaker(s) should be the one (s) impeached. Recall the "Vision for the Philippine Judiciary" emblazoned on court walls: "A judiciary that is independent, effective and efficient, and worthy of public trust and confidence."

Saguisag & Associates Lawyers 4045 Bigasan Street, Palanan 1235 Makati Office

oooooo

13

Thank you, Senator Fulbright; on being full of oneself
Undated, circa 2018

Kudos! Debating was one activity I was involved in, as a stude.

Below, my Times piece last Friday, just in case you have no copy yet, the paper having come out on Good Friday.***** I hope the San Beda Law Faculty Development Program will have a resurrection. Maybe it hath not been dead, only it hath slumbered.

Thank you, Senator Fulbright; on being full of oneself

I DON'T recall ever having a column published on Good Friday, which the pious usually spend repenting. But, today, you are holding a copy of the best paper in town. A mild surprise?

A culture shocker for me was my having to be in a classroom on Good Friday, in 1968, at Harvard Law. The reason I got there was that in 1967, Fr. Alex Mari Ganuza, College of Law Prefect of San Beda, instituted a Faculty Development Program, with me as the first awardee. I had not thought of foreign studies earlier, for lack of means but that program had me writing to various schools, including Harvard Law, which quickly responded with an offer of a full scholarship ($4,100, big money at the time). Still, the unaffordable cost of travel deterred me. San Beda's P15,000 could cover it but what about the family I helped support?

The Fulbright program, on my application, came to my rescue, like a cavalry horse answering the bugle.

Last Friday evening, we had a delightful 70th anniversary celebration of its Philippine program at the Manila Pen (I have long wondered why a hotel in Makati is so called. And our contronyms: "salvage" means to save or have some pulis patola send someone to the Promised Land). I didn't have to touch the San Beda money at all but left it to cover our bunso's transfer to San Beda High from Pasig Catholic.

I think it was only this paper that had carried news of what was coming last Friday. And the other day, a columnist in another paper, wrote glowingly of his own Fulbright experience. Good news not newsworthy?

Gala dinner I arrived at the Pen a little late and was escorted to a table where awardee Cora Santos de la Paz-Bernardo was seated, next to hubby Ike Bernardo. She was salutatorian and Ike was first honorable mention in their Pasig Rizal Hi Class'56 (I was in '55). Cora hailed from Pateros, a younger sister of my classmate, Josie, also very bright and beautiful. In the table next to ours was honoree Joey V. Cuisia, with wife Vicky, both of whom would consult me on matters legal long, long ago. How time has flown.

Cora, No. 1 in the CPA exams, attended Cornell. We were two promdis privileged to go to the Ivy League. Perhaps, to the shock of some of my Section 1 classmates. Although I had finished grade school in Makati Elem in five years(accelerated) and would occasionally make the Rizal Hi honor roll, I was described in the latter's school organ graduation issue as a "galawgaw: with a boy's will to turn somersault."

The other honorees in that Fulbright Philippines 70th Anniversary Gala Dinner – Reflections on 70 years of Excellence night, were: Angel C. Alcala, Bienvenido L. Lumbera, Bienvenido F. Nebres, S. J., Clare R. Baltazar, Napoleon V. Abueva, Abdulmari Asia Imao, Lucrecia R. Kasilag and Conchita M. Abad, in the order their names appeared in the program. Joey was No. 2, Cora was No. 3 and I was No. 6. Gems of purest ray serene, a phrase I picked up as a high school junior, from Gray's haunting Elegy, which has stayed with me, giving me a sense of where I am.

Thank you, Senator Fulbright. Thank you, Ambassador Kim, for a lovely way to spend a fun evening.

It was SRO. Sen Ed Angara, a man of many parts, and feats, was in the table of Ambassadors Kim and Joey. Ben Muego, a feared debater in our time, came by to say hello. So did Baby Baua, my late Dulce's Girl Friday in many a project. And many others, including one who told a daughter-in- law of mine, Judge Jackie, who texted her congrats and asked why I had not told my nuke family. It had not occurred to me to do so, a habit from time out of mind.

Rizal High reminiscences. Rizal High has also produced Jovito Salonga, Neptali Gonzales, Bobbit Sanchez, Lucio San Pedro, Botong Francisco and Pat and Wilma Tiamzon, said to head the New People's Army. The couple are out on bail, and I am a guarantor or bondsman. Cora and Ike did not mix in high school. She is from Pateros, while Ike is my fellow BatamPasig. The Pateros and Pasig Mafias engaged in a healthy rivalry. Cora married Pat de la Paz, from Colegio de San Agustin in Iloilo, who bar-reviewed in San Beda in 1963. He was No. 3 among 5,500 examinees, with 85.05 (I was only No. 6, with 84.85). He passed away in 1995, after serving in government with distinction. After more than a decade, Cora and Ike had a reunion, in matrimony.

I was a nothing HS grad but I was always in Section 1 and occasionally made the honor roll.

However, our hambog barkada thought that being seen studying was disgraceful, haha. And were we bullied and insulted by teachers telling us to go home and plant camote. On rainy days we'd go to school in bakya. We were bulakbuleros who just enjoyed life in high school, and learned who Herodotus' son was, "history" being its father. We'd be ambushed by teachers who, from out of the blue, would ask us to spell "picturesque," etc.

In January 1955, Eddie Sanchez, bunso in Bobbit's brood of seven, our valedictorian, and I were playing hooky, in Quiapo. We saw extras blaring the 1-2 finish of San Beda in the 1954 bar, which I read as pointing me to that school (also, fare to and from Legarda was 15 centavos, beyond that 20). I was not to study hard until sophomore law when I was in the middle of many co-curricular commitments, in the National Union of Students and Student Catholic Action, teaching catechism at Mapa High just across, writing, debating, extempo speaking, partying, and emerging as college chess champ and member of champion softball (I was second baseman and contributed) and basketball (best seat in the house, the bench, which I warmed) intrams teams.

Pat and Wilma Tiamzon graduated with honors, who could have qualified for Fulbright, but, in their eyes, they preferred the harder right to the easier wrong (West Point prayer), loving their country with that kind of passion that whips the blood (Fred Reinfeld). They rebelled not long after the Marcoses moved to Malacañang when Macoy opened his William Saunders account, and Imelda, her Jane Ryan's, in Switzerland.

Crime   pays?
Marcos and Duterte
          Cooperation among the Swiss, the Americans and ourselves made possible the transfer of the kleptocratic loot in the billions while blood flowed, but nothing like what has flooded the streets after Digong won. A bloodbath. Given the Yamashita/Medina standard of command responsibility, Digong does not want to take part in the International Criminal Court proceeding, given the little risk of winning.

          After martial law was inflicted, Marcos had his arrest, search and seizure orders (ASSOs). But, today, Digong casually orders the arrest of people like the Dimple bus owner and PUV colorum operators, arguably usurping the function of prosecutors and judges. The former conduct preliminary investigations and the latter conduct probable-cause determinations, now erased by Digong, a super-executive, super-court, super-legislature and a one-man continuing constitutional convention, doing all the work. He seems to have a messianic complex, and those who get in his way, like hief Justice Meilou, who fights for judicial independence, find themselves   in   a   pickle.
There is a debate on what a dynasty is. I know that Prez Digong Duterte, Mayor Sara Duterte and Vice Mayor Pulong Duterte comprised a dynasty (Pulong has since resigned). Justice Potter Stewart despaired of his inability to define "obscenity" but in the end triumphantly said: "I know   it   when   I   see   it."
Cardinal Tagle said last Sunday: "In our world today, we have many kings, full of arrogance,

lacking in humility, in our time; many of us follow kings who use violence, arms, threats, clearly showing lack of understanding and solidarity with the weak." Sino naman po kaya ang pinatatamaan? Holmes said even a dog can tell if it is being kicked or stumbled over.

Palace tutas do not see their boss as being alluded to, as the administration supposedly does not go after the innocent. And who plays god and passes judgment and discards the presumption of innocence? Some tutas may be smarter, and may acknowledge quietly that the Philippines is indeed part of "our world today." The Cardinal was talking of other places? C'mon.

May Digong this week—belated Happy Birthday, truly—do as he correctly says, piously, of Lent, not what he incorrectly does, impiously, elsewhere, at other times.

Anyway, this Sunday, Happy Easter everyone!

Saguisag & Associates Lawyers 4045 Bigasan Street, Palanan 1235 Makati Office Nos. (+632) 551-6350/833- 4140 Fax No. (+632) 831-2276

oooooo

14

SALNS In A Scofflaw Society

Mar 21, 2018

"Biggest Batch of Women Cadets to Greet DU30," read a headline, referring to the new women PMAyers. I made possible the entry of women into the PMA in a 1991 bicameral committee conferenceon Women in Nation Building - authored by my college chum, Raul S. Roco - R.A. No. 7192. (A bicam meet is conducted when the two chambers' differing versions need to be harmonized, or enhanced, making that body that powerful, as the Third House. I simply had the sex requirement deleted..

There is of course the Fourth House, the Camara de la Imprenta, where it is said a naughty lawmaker would add a zero or two at the end to a budget, say, for an Avenue, hehe.

I trust General Florencio Magsino has forgiven me by now for fathering the breach in the last bastion of machismo, to last and even > spread. Last time we met some years ago, he was still chiding me, for my impertinence.

The chauvinist Prez and the times may have not been kind to women like Senator Leila de Lima, Ombudsman Chit Carpio-Morales, journalists Maria Ressa/Pia Ranada, CHED chief Tatti Licuanan, and Chief Justice (CJ) Meilou Sereneo, for standing up to the Prez, whose expansionary appetite seems boundless. He wants total control of the government and the press. But, these gutsy undiscourageable women, like Ka Celing Muñoz Palma, doggedly soldier on.

The marathon House (of arguably namby-pamby Tutas?) hearings may finally end but then there's the remarkable and unexpected quo warranto (QW) proceeding filed by the Solicitor General, Joe Calida. All along, the talk had been of R.A. No. 6713, until Cong. Vicente Veloso (former Court of Appeals Justice) triggered a Eureka! moment in the Lower House, and in the SolGen's QW petition, Compañero Joe unexpectedly hammered on R.A. No. 3019, thusly: "80. The SALN requirement in the Charter recognized what has already been in the statute books. As early as 1960, Congress imposed that requirement in R.A. No. 3019. Section 7 of the law according states: "Section 7. Statement of assets and liabilities. Every public officer, within thirty days . . . after assuming office, and within the month of January of every other year thereafter, as well as upon the expiration of his term of office, or upon his resignation or separation from office, shall prepare and file with the office of the corresponding Department Head, or in the case of a Head of Department or chief of an independent office, with the Office of the President, or in the case of members of the Congress and the officials and employees thereof, with the Office of the Secretary of the corresponding House, a true detailed and sworn statement of assets and liabilities, including A STATEMENT OF THE AMOUNTS AND

SOURCES OF HIS INCOME, THE AMOUNTS OF HIS PERSONAL AND FAMILY EXPENSES AND THE AMOUNT OF INCOME TAXES PAID FOR THE NEXT PRECEDING CALENDAR YEAR: . . . . (Caps added.)*

Interesting. If the SolGen can show me an authentic copy of a statement timely filed by him or any other incumbent where the filer disclosed THE AMOUNTS AND SOURCES OF HIS INCOME, THE AMOUNTS OF HIS PERSONAL AND FAMILY EXPENSES AND THE AMOUNT OF INCOME TAXES PAID FOR THE NEXT PRECEDING CALENDAR YEAR, I'll eat it.*

The Good Book has something to say about seeing the mote in one's eyes and missing the beam in one's own. Joe's 17 assistants who co-signed his petition may save their boss and themselves by showing us copies of their own SALNs complying with the Tolentino Law to show that we are not entirely a nation of scofflaws, or fake pretentious

Tribunes. All these years, I have challenged my studes to produce a SALN complying not only with R.A. No. 6713 (the Salonga-Saguisag Law), but also with R.A. No. 3019. Only one, a woman stude of mine, seems to have succeeded as to the latter but it was one preserved by the filer from the Dark Years; I passed her on that *fantastic * *basis alone.*

In 2012, the Civil Service Commission (CSC), the lead agency under Sec. 12 of R.A. No. 6713, tried to enforce Sec. 7 of R.A. No. 3019; the Lower (bagay talaga) House howled. The CSC was seen scampering away with its tail between its legs. Natameme. CSC, how about it, today?

The law hath not been dead though it hath slept? Shakespeare's Measure for Measure.

I have always stressed that our intent in passing R.A. No. 6713 was administrative, not criminal. Thus, a vital provision is Sec. 10, on a > Review and Compliance Procedure, for correction.

Lead agency is the civil Civil Service Commission, not the punitive Ombudsman nor the Department of Justice.

What I have been suggesting is for Congress to amnesty the massive noncompliance, to benefit Presidents down to the last Barangay dogcatcher, with the caveat that thereafter, violators would be dealt with more severely, particularly lawyers.

My pal, Mon Tulfo, not a lawyer, says to qualify as a state witness, one must be "the least guilty," PDI, 3/20/18, and who therefore may know nothing or little then, so, whatever for? What Sec. 17 (e) of Rule 119 of the Rules of Court really says is the "accused does not appear to be the most guilty," but may know a lot of criminatory stuff.

On another pal Oscar Lagman's questioning in the same PDI issue the grant of bail to nonagenarian JPE, the Supreme Court, in 1946, granted bail for humanitarian reasons to Benigno Aquino, Sr., in 1947; he passed away the following year, at 47, watching a boxing match in Rizal Memorial. Uncle Jovy Salonga was released by Macoy to the custody of Auntie Lydia, a prisoner of love.

Last JPE and I shook hands in the Senate, where we were for Manang Letty Ramos-

Shahani's necro, his grip was firm and he indeed looked

ma-kamandag pa. Bedroom terrorist still? Indeed, how many can boast of at least 38 girlfriends, as reported in the Inquirer some years ago, if my memory is true? And counting? Frail, and deserving of release, was he, according to doctors in the Supreme Court? You're telling me. Now, he'll prosecute, vigorously.

Tough Manong JPE may be a bull-strong lead prosecutor in the trial of CJ Meilou Sereno, whom SolGen Joe Calida charged for allegedly not filing a statement under Sec. 7 of R.A. No. 3019, again, on "the amounts and sources of [her] income, the amounts of [her] personal and family expenses and the amount of income taxes paid for the next preceding calendar year." Petition, pp. 28-29. Heretofore, talk was limited to R.A. No. 6713. Now, the SolGen brought in R.A. No. 3019, and he may yet live to regret it. Again, if the feisty SolGen and his 17 assistants, all competent, who co-signed the Quo Warranto petition can show me copies of their statements mentioning said income, expenses and taxes, I'll eat them.

Not to miss the beams in one's own eyes, when pointing out the motes in others'. Such awfully sanctimonious piece of pious fiction in a country where laws are "more honored in the breach, than in the observance." Hamlet.

Anyone charged is entitled to a fair and impartial tribunal. How many Justices have prejudged the CJ and prematurely thrown their weight on the other side? Can they sit in judgment of one they have publicly condemned? It is hornbook doctrine that even if a rule be fair on its face but if it is administered with an evil eye and an unequal hand, it would violate one's basic human and constitutional right to equal protection. Yick Wo v. Hopkins, 118 U.S. 356, 373-74 (1886).

Justice must satisfy the appearance of justice? How many Justices have held their horses while evidence trickles in of some allegedly impeachable offense? whatever may be proven in regard to the Tolentino Law of 1960 and the Salonga-Saguisag Law of 1989, an impeachable offense is respectfully submitted to be out, more so if the review-and-complian ce requirement is not met.

And the unprecedented appearance in the House to make sumbong and the public statements of those who may not like the CJ, who may arguably need Dale Carnegie lessons, may come back to haunt them. They answer to their conscience and to history.

I hope to see a better Supreme Court focused on deciding cases - a lofty constitutional task - not frittering away their time in forlorn time- and energy-wasting turf struggles, dividing, and weakening the judiciary, to the delight of an irredentist presidency. But, even if so focused, decisions only seem to reflect the prevailing power situation, when and where the Palace is interested in.

That is the sin of the CJ, not kowtowing, and saying, "Yes, Master." If she had behaved like the Lower House supernumerary ooops, super-majority, she would not be impeached by the House and tried by the Senate, much less "quo-warrantiz ed", to borrow from a law classmate who floored Prof. Florenz Regalado, with his neology.

Saguisag & Associates Lawyers 4045 Bigasan Street, Palanan 1235 Makati Office Nos. (+632) 551-6350 <+63%202% 20551%206350/833-4140 Fax No. (+632) 831-2276 <+63%202% 20831%202276>

oooooo

15
"Mon Ami, You've to Start Somewhere"

Feb. 28, 2018

The February 10, 2018 issue of the Daily Inquirer bannered: "DU3T to Int'l Court: Why start with me? President Duterte questions the ICC [Int'l Criminal Court] decision to start its preliminary examination of alleged crimes against humanity in Asia with him when `massacres' are occurring in many other countries in the region."

Why do Frenchmen kiss a woman's hand? In 1986, in a breakfast meeting we had in Manila Hotel with Secretary of State George Shultz, he recounted this answer of a Frenchman: "Mon ami, you have to start somewhere."

The defense of selective prosecution, unequal protection or invidious discrimination will only work, if shown that "justice" is maladministered with an evil eye and an unequal hand.

But for Digong, there's always the risk of winning of course, by mounting a credible vigorous defense.

It is no defense "though"" that so many robberies are occurring anyway so why single out suspect John Doe? And here, there may be other damaging facts.

Only last August, 32 were killed in one day, in Bulacan, in the anti-poor war against drugs. An ecstatic Malacañang, perhaps concerned over our population explosion situation, said Kill-Pa-More. Digong is the only one in the region bragging about his population production program, which no one has copied in dealing with a drug problem going back beyond a century [not only during PNoy's watch, believe you me].

Digong's idol, Marcos, would deny, deny, deny. Or at least, dissemble. Macoy knew that fish is caught by its mouth but he lost anyway in Switzerland, Honolulu and Seattle. Billions were returned as ill-gotten wealth after the July 15, 2003 decision of the Supreme Court, which inexplicably did not order the prosecution of the "ill-gotteners ". The Marcoses are now where they are, working furiously for their Restoration, emboldened by Macoy's transfer to the LMB (damaged and downgraded in my view to Libingan ng mga Mandarambong at Berdugo).

As PNP head Bato de la Rosa, equally very talkative, said, his men now would he "more responsible" , after being pulled out from the back burner. Was the abandoned original Tokhang "responsible" at all? Why the pull-out "then" (which could also harm Digong in the ICC)?

To me, unlamented by the Church and the human rights community, and perceived as "irresponsible ," bloody and messy, the failed policy indicates why it was abandoned, reacting to local and global outrage. The PNP (Pulis Na Patolas) was told to back off. Too many of the poorest of the poor had died. Now the ICC has taken notice, and not improperly, from where I sit.

A state-sanctioned crime against the poor is not a crime against humanity?

The revised PNP program is an admission that the bloody messy program of dealing with a century-old problem, which no country has aped, had been a colossal failure, resulting in the death of the poorest of the many who are poor. Now, I shift to a friend who is not poor but whose heart is very much in the right place.

Again flavor of the week is my very dear friend, Loida Nicolas-Lewis, a "pal" of my youth. Last Monday we had lunch in Vicky Garchitorena's place. Tatti Licuanan, Lirio Covey, Yoly Fenix, Bert Fenix, Sonia Malasarte-Roco, and Ditas Rivera-da Silva attended. (The next night, Solaire, some re-assembled, to dancexercise in the hotel's Eclipse.)

Our thoughts were with Loida, who is unwelcome in Davao City. *Personae non gratae*, along with Sen. Sonny Trillanes. Why? Knowing her, she fights intensely for what is right and prevails by the force of reason, not by reason of force. EJKs don't amuse her.

Presidents have to thrive in a hardy climate, "and" not be *balat sibuyas.*

Loida has been a friend since college days. Then it turned out that Reggie Lewis, her would-be husband, and I, were in the Harvard Law graduating class in 1968. In 1998, Loida funded my travelling and joining our 30th anniversary reunion (full disclosure). I am incredulous at what Digong and Davaoenos have thought and done to her, and Senator Sonny. Yup, *personae non gratae*. No fair.

We should have room not only for brown-nosing Mocha Usons but also for those whose thoughts we may disagree with, and indeed even despise, in a robust democracy. More democratic space, not less.

In 1967, "my only" sister finished in UP (two engineering degrees) and I attended the graduation rites in Diliman. Among the graduands were best friends Loida and Violy Calvo (gone, the first wife of Senator Frank Drilon).

Former serious Student Catholic Action stalwarts would not go out of the law to oppose. Loida credibly denies Digong's charge that she was

behind the ICC case against Digong.

I have reason to believe that all of us now into our second adolescence are respectful of human rights and against extrajudicial killing. Maybe even judicial killing. Or even killing one, softly.

SSS chief Dean Amado Valdez and Commissioner Pompee La Viña deserved better than being killed softly, fired unceremoniously.

Infighting? I see nothing wrong with creative tension in itself. But, the way Digong arrogantly mishandles dismissals is sad, leading to misperception.

He has to try to be kinder and gentler. A little ceremony recognizing the two for having done their tasks well would have been better. Tatti Licuanan's departure could also have been done in a better way. Too many foreign trips? It looks to me she has justified each one..

Tourism Secretary Wanda Teo may justify her many foreign trips but, with a make-up artist (per the Star)? However, with a courageous and influential brother in Mon Tulfo, she won't get the Tatti treatment.

While the other day was special(Ash Wednesday and Valentine), I'd prefer to cite Digong's repetition of the demand to return the Bells of Balangiga. But now, two U.S. Congressmen object unless there is some improvement in the situation posed by the bloody, messy anti-poor war against drugs.

What can I say? Digong, Bato, you have to start somewhere. At Mass the other evening in spacious San Isidro in Pasay, I saw emblazoned HUWAG KANG PAPATAY. An apt writing on the wall. Nice to have a sweet comic funny Valentine but not to forget that dust we all are, and to dust we all shall return.

oooooo

16

EDSA's Revisionism; Fallacies

Feb 28, 2018

The intriguing appointment of Ka Eduardo Manalo of the INC as special envoy raises serious questions on separation of church and state and whether he should also file his SALN (Statement of Assets, Liabilities, Net Worth, etc.). That was my intent in sponsoring R.A. No. 6713, the Code of Conduct and Ethical Standards, benefiting from the groundwork laid down by the UP College of Public Administration, on which principal author Uncle Jovy Salonga had relied (Uncle, again, cuz my lola and his mother were first cousins in a Pasig looban).

Sec. 3(B) of the Code defines "public officials" to include "appointive officials.... permanent or temporary, whether in the career or non-career service, . . . whether or not they receive compensation, regardless of amount." Arguable? Abangan. The Supreme Court may say my intent in the legislative arena meant nothing.

All of us who have war stories of Edsa'86, whose 32nd anniversary we just marked, have validated what the spouses Durants wrote: all autobiography is vanity.

On February 22, 1986, Juan Ponce Enrile (JPE), a genuine Edsa'86 hero, said in what sounded like a death-bed confession or dying declaration that he had cheated for Macoy by 300,000 votes in Cagayan earlier that month and that his supposed September 22, 1972 ambuscade was fake news, making skeptics give him the benefit of a lingering doubt that it was all a zarzuela to nail Cory.

To her and to us who were at Edsa beginning September 23, 1972, Edsa'86 validated that while we are grateful to JPE, FVR, Joe Almonte, Eugene Ocampo, Gringo, and the institutional parliament (Batasang Pambansa), it in fact represented the triumph of what we boycotters called the Parliament of the Streets. We were MPs (Mambabatas Panlansangan).

MABINI was among the eleven petitioners which had questioned the constitutionality of the snap polls; the Supreme Court said on December 19, 1985 that no, the show must go on, as it were (in a nation crazy about elections, whether for Prez or Binibining Palanggana).

Doy Laurel's role cannot be minimized but it was a fact that the Laurels were in bed with Macoy from 1972 to 1980, when he joined us and added sterling gravitas to our effort. Earlier businessmen Jimmy Ongpin openly, and Al Yuchengco, furtively, had joined the determined opposition redemocratization efforts.

We copied Portugal' s Carnation Revolution of April 1974, also involving colonels and civvies lasting likewise for four days with women putting carnations in the muzzle of guns, which unfortunately for the Portuguese did not have the benefit of cable television.

Has Edsa'86 failed? No overthrow of authoritarianism can be a failure, from where I sit.

Cory would openly admit that Ninoy was not the worst victim of martial law but just happened to be the most prominent. Business, which would make money even if blood was flowing in the streets (Baron Rotschild), realized that no one was safe after August 21, 1983, when Ninoy was salvaged on landing (validating Tita Aurora's "kutob ng ina", concurred in only Dr. Guy J. Pauker of a think tank - Rand); we know-it-alls dismissed the possibility in a huge meet in the home of Esto and Maur Lichauco on August 7, 1983.

Makati Business had its confetti canyons, matched in Davao by a Yellow Friday group led by the mother of Digong and therefore he could not just kick all Yellows in the teeth, out of affection and respect for his beloved mom, another genuine Edsa'86 hero. Dilawan, forever. I *am* a Yellow, and proud of it, and always will.

Anyway, Digong should really watch his language, stop bitching that his pay is not enough for his two wives (and kulasisis?) - unpresidential - and do something about the traffic situation. Not trivial at all; we are said to lose P3.5B daily cause of the traffic. But, more critical, he has also arguably violated the Constitution in an impeachable way by allowing the erection of military installations by China in the West Philippine Sea. Not enough to be dismissive about it it that anyway the missiles would not be directed at us but at America, where millions of Pinoy, not only Loida Nicolas-Lewis, have migrated. How many have, to China?

After we Malevolent/Magnific ent Twelve ended our status as America' s last plantation in 1991, "foreign military bases, troops, or facilities shall not [be] allowed in the Philippines except under a treaty concurred in by the Senate and when the Congress so requires, ratified by a majority of the votes cast by the people in a national referendum held for that purpose, and recognized as a treaty by the other contracting State." 1987 Const., Art. XVIII, Sec. 25. But, our Congress, reminiscent of what Mark Twain said, that the only distinct American criminal class is Congress, is too busy to be bothered by what is going on in the West Philippine Sea.

I credit the Star's Dik Pascual for the above insight on a seemingly impeachable offense far worse than has appeared so far in the allegations to unseat Chief Justice Meilou Sereno (not the one I endorsed in 2012 but she was chosen in a totally constitutional manner; I am appreciative of her writing finis to the case of Lenny Villa, killed on Feb. 11, 1991, which lasted 25 years, a long time for client Zos Mendoza to be anxious; also, for her joining in another well-written separate concurring opinion the ruling acquitting another former client of mine, Hubert Webb, on December 14, 2010). After what's going on, will we have the same Supreme Court, or stronger, or weaker (given Digong's transparent interest in removing someone who has crossed him)?

I wish they would simply heed the spirit of nominee Byron White's response when asked in the U.S. Senate how he envisioned his role would be as a Justice: "To decide cases."

Not to share administrative power and other distractions, given the SC's thousands of pending cases.

In January 1987, I, 47, turned down a signed Supreme Court appointment. I am a psycho with head not properly and tightly screwed on? Another proof that I was sira was that I wrote for Dik's opposition paper pre-Edsa' 86, with his wife picking up my copy Sunday afternoons.

Spousal heroes.

Digong has Chinese blood, like many of us, and he might not overly mind our becoming the 24th province of China, as he has suggested (jocosely?), but watch what he does, not what he says, haz lo que hago, no lo que digo). A referendum however may show more votes for our becoming the 51st State; I cannot imagine though why the U.S. would welcome 107M poor conejos. We do not, like Maria Clara, throw ourselves at the U.S.

If a small woman is raped by the brawny burly Barangay bully and resistance would seem futile should she not simply yield physically but resist spiritually? For this intriguing idea, the late actor Rod Navarro introed me in Pasig to the books of Donald Hamilton (Rod was a wide reader, and would not use camel when he could employ "dromedary. " We played pinball in Pasig and ballroom-dancexerci sed in Manila's Alegria and Makati's Bahia, both gone now.

Fellow Bedan Justice Sammy Martires in a remarkable intriguing ponencia says "we simply cannot be stuck to the Maria Clara stereotype of a demure and reserved Filipino woman." Hmmmmm.

You be the judge, in general. Each case though must be decided in its factual context. In Club Nautilus on Dewey (now Roxas) Blvd., also gone, it was said that the men were naughty and the girls were loose. Happy hours.

What is definitely sad in the current administration is the continuing use of the Nazi salute, illegal in some countries, topped by argumentum ad hominem, baculum et populum. Judged on language (bastos and unkind), dynasties (Dutertes, Prez, Mayor and Vice Mayor, the latter now ex-), traffic, rice shortage or hoarding, and rising prices, it has been a total failure thus far.

Can we really say corruption has been reduced and the police are more respected than dreaded?

We can all learn from Tolstoy and West Point, that good people change others, better people change the system (parliamentary/ presidential federal) but the best ones change, themselves. West Point cadets pray for them to prefer the harder right instead of the easier wrong and never to settle for a half truth when the whole can be won.

oooooo

17
Confucius and the Inevitability of Rape

Feb 7, 2018

If rape is inevitable, lie back and enjoy it." When my long-time and valued friend, Foreign Affairs Secretary Raul Manglapus, said it, he got thrashed-talk all over the place. In fact, I had heard it often before, from various sources. Indeed, my ultimate source is Confucius (born 551 B.C.?), from China, a country of very smart and shrewd people.

Napoleon was right, when the sleeping giant (China) awoke, the world would tremble. We are trembling now, aren't we? Or "lying supinely on our backs" - in the words of Patrick Henry in his 1775 "give me liberty or give me death!" speech (Prof. Ipe Dino made us memorize and recite it as freshmen in San Beda).

China has effectively and subtly taken over the disputed isles in the West Philippine Sea. The administration falls all over itself in rationalizing and speaking for China, which cleverly lets its local arguably caponized spokesmen do all the work. The new twist is Presidential Spokesperson Harry Roque now plays the Blame Game and thrashes PNoy, who has been out of power for 20 months. Assuming softie PNoy were to account, when rape first was first attempted, he resisted by going to an arbitral tribunal (where my pal, Paul Reichler, who attended Harvard and trained in Arnold & Porter, as I had done earlier - won. He had also beaten in the World Court his own native U.S.A., for Nicaragua, which ruling the former ignored until there was a regime change years later, when Violeta Chamorro took over. I am verifying whether some settlement was reached. Paul and I had worked together, in another matter, for our government).

What have toughies Digong and Harry done? Jetski? Lie back and enjoy being deflowered? Or as fair Laetitia did, prevent being raped by Fireblood by giving her timely consent? Again and again, the new regime has consented. *Alalaong baga kung saan nadapa duon tumihaya?*

PNoy and Digong have Chinese blood. And so does Cardinal Tagle. And so did Cardinal Sin and Rizal. And how many of us can really say we do not have a smidgen of it? Are we ripe and ready to be super-bully China's 24th province? Digong and his advisers had better reassure us that it ain't so in the same manner that we are leery of being America' s last plantation. But, the administration dissembles, not only as to China.

Digong mow says he is for a "hybrid" form of government, whatever that means. A hybrid government for a mongrelized nation? Askals? Asong Kalye. But every dog, it is said, has its day. Will we?

Last Saturday, it was Lions day, and night, in Mendiola as Bedans came home, from all over. When I came in early that evening, certain senior alums on stage belted out the rousing sing-able The Red and The White, the origin of which I have not been able to trace and which has since been discarded in the NCAA, sadly.

At 78, last August, I, a Leo, seemed to have been the oldest alum among those who attended the Mendiola reunion, now in our Second Adolescence. OK, older was Fr. Benildus Maramba, OSB - which we used to say stood for Order of Society Boys, party animals; he is my first cousin-in-law, who quickly gave me another Rosario on first contact. Other alums may have left early when the night was still young, mayhap to be with their lovely Rosarios elsewhere.

This week, our paper carried pages from the past on the drug (opium) problem in the Philippines in the 1930's when our Guv-Gen was Chester Davis (the famed and coveted Davis Cup in tennis was named after him). At this time, we note how ancient the drug problem is and there are reports on how vicious Fentanyl could be. Prez Digong acknowledges using it as a pain-killer. It is also a people-killer. See "Fentanyl kills 16 in English city," Phil. Star, Feb. 5, 2018, p. 15, col. 5. So careful, Mr. Prez, we wish you well and pray that you change in some ways, and succeed, "for our good and the good of all His church [our people]".

The Manila Times of February 3, 1930, p.1 (page or blast from the past), as reprinted here last Saturday, recounted that a League of Nations

Opium Mission arrived that morning, to "interfere," what else? The body was composed of two Swedes, a Belgian, a Czech and a Brit. The party was met on board by a PC Colonel, who did not denounce the interference, and in fact brought the party to Malaca¤ang. Today, Digong and Bato de la Rosa would tell a similar mission where to go. Not to China, where shabu (worth billions) apparently continues to come, through our porous shorelines.

Guv-Gen Davis placed at the visitors' disposal the government's facilities for assistance. It had been formed at the instance of the British government and its ultimate purpose was to help devise legislation to lessen the evils of drug trafficking. The commission had visited ten places and would visit five more and thence to Geneva about the middle of April 1930. That night, Davis gave a Palace banquet in honor of the commission dealing with a long-time problem. Ambeth Ocampo wrote in the Inquirer in April 2016 that Rizal tried Mary Jane (marijuana).

As I also said here in 2016, Tibo Mijares wrote in the Conjugal Dictatorship: "[Y.S.] Kwong made the stunning revelation that Josefa Edralin [Macoy's Ma] was arrested in Arellano High School for having opium and heroin in her possession. Kwong even mentioned the name of the arresting officer as Telesforo Tenorio, then a detective but later . . . a chief of police of Manila. The suspicion was that Josefa was selling drugs to the students of the school where she was a teacher and librarian. According to Kwong,

Josefa was able to either bribe or cry her way of out the incident." Page 257.

Speaking of American Guv-Gens, we also should recall at this time of year Frank Murphy, as we mark Manila's liberation in February 1945. After him was named what is now known as Camp Aguinaldo. Murphy was the last U.S. Guv-Gen here, the last one, as a Justice, I would have thought would take the side of Yamashita when his case reached the U.S. Supreme Court. I emotionally and heatedly blasted Yamashita in our class in Harvard Law in 1967-68, to my classmate' resounding approval - they applauded; it took me decades to realize the wisdom of not succumbing to the high feelings of the moment for in the sober afterglow we may realize the sorry implications of emotionalized Fire! Aim! Ready! crusades. This I seem to see in the current Dengxavia controversy. Clint Eastwood' s sage advice is for one to know his limitations. Medical expertise is not universal, on autopsies, a distinct specialty.

Last Tuesday, I saw here a pix of Mayor Erap Estrada and Veep Leni Robredo marking the Liberation of Manila, a bloody month-long (Feb. 3 to Mar. 3, 1945) episode in which 100,000 were killed south of the Pasig. Admiral Sanji Iwabuchi (when defeat was imminent, he committed suicide,
said in Japan to be the sincerest form of apology; unknown here, masakit yata) was in command of 12,000 Marines. But, it was Tomoyuki Yamashita, who had lost communication and control over his 4,000 soldiers, who was executed; he was up

north in the bloody month-long battle. It gave rise to the controversial Yamashita Standard of command responsibility. That may also be the Nuremberg Standard, thanks to Hitler.

But getting more and more widespread is the use of the Hitler-Duterte salute, with fists thrust forward. This was standard and expected of Hitler's storm troopers, the reason Aussie Spymaster Nick Warner got pummelled and pilloried from pillar to post for doing the fist bump with Digong. Our own people are either too scared or too ignorant not to to be lemmings. Fellow Bedans are ignorant?

Anyway, a son told me last Tuesday San Beda is now a university.(?) When I entered San Beda, in 1955, a promdi from Pasig, it was but a small college, but like Daniel Webster, speaking of Dartmouth, I say, there were those of us who loved it, and always will.

There I learned much about fierce Muslim warriors who never submitted to Imperial Manila; this may be an argument why there is martial law in Mindanao, and always will, or should, according to the Supreme Court, if I read correctly its latest excrescence, from where I sit, as a fervent student of human rights.

--

Saguisag & Associates Lawyers 4045 Bigasan Street, Palanan 1235 Makati Office Nos. (+632) 551-6350/833-4140 Fax No. (+632) 831 2276.

ooooo

18
Chacha in a Scofflaw Nation

Jan. 31, 2018

So ex-Customs Chief Nicanor Faeldon is now a Batang City Jail (BJC) candidate-member, in Pasay. There we visited Doy Laurel midnight of February 17, 1984 when he was arrested for alleged illegal possession of a gun. Maverick Judge Dionisio Capistrano dismissed the case the next day, a Saturday. We were 42 lawyers, led by Ka Celing Muñoz Palma, Soc Rodrigo and Paddy Padilla. We argued that the gun had been planted (good that on dismissal, no one suggested that we ask for the gun's "return, " haha. Doy, a hero but, muy pillo).

I was a BCJ candidate-member myself in early 1983, in Quezon City, not good enough for ABC, Aguinaldo, Bonifacio-Bicutan and Crame. On February 4, 1983 Judge Jose Castro jailed me cuz I had allegedly "arrogantly announced that President Ferdinand E. Marcos is a super-subversive . . . ." and "this is now the second offense of contempt [I] committed" . Fined P50.00 earlier for bitching that the court was getting militarized given the presence of so many uniforms I said, "I' d gladly pay it, Your Honor," pulling out a hundred-peso bill, and asked, "may I say something more for another fifty pesos?" He changed the subject cuz I was loony even then.

There in Pasay also I visited Gina Doe in the mid-90s. She had retained me by phone patch, over Radio Veritas, one early morning. She had been accused of mutilating John Doe, her lover who napped in their motel room, after telling her their affair was over; his wife was coming home from abroad as a contract worker. The bobo awoke, yelling in pain, feeling very much diminished. The woman, a modista, always had a pair of scissors in her bag. Case dismissed by Judge Aurora Reciña. The Tsikboy simply got tired of appearing in court with a towel wrapped around his head and hearing, "iyan ang naputulan." We invoked denial of a speedy trial. His manhood had become Exh. E, in a bottle.

As I understand it, in the U.S.. Congress may not detain anyone, unless it first secures an arrest order from a court when the resource person refuses to talk, invoking the 5th, even after assurance of immunity. Courts routinely cooperate. A test case may be needed here lest Faeldon be detained until the cows come home.

Last week the cows came home for Tony Cortes, my law classmate, who will miss our emerald anniv program tomorrow in San Beda. The friends of one's youth are the finest one can ever have, to paraphrase Robert Penn Warren in All The King's Men. Tony was a good lawyer who was with nationalist Abe Sarmiento, for decades, before the latter joined the Supreme Court.

Last Sunday, I attended the Sto. Niño march-procession in Mendiola; for the first time ever, I couldn't complete it. We're ageing and ailing and current events can only aggravate our condition. Such as Rappler's fate. Its true unforgivable crime is being critical of the Prez. Had it been brown-nosing Digong, Maria Ressa, like blogger Mocha Uson, might have even been invited to accompany him on his trips abroad. Thus, a conundrum.

When you reach a fork in the road, take it, NY Yankee Yogi Berra's sage advice I am reminded of cuz of the weird insistence that PNoy be charged with reckless imprudence resulting in homicide for Mamasapano; the latter offense does not involve malice or moral turpitude. I became a widower cuz of reckless driving, upping my familiarity with it.

A reckless imprudence accused is entitled to probation on conviction, for "mere" recklessness, no matter how painful the consequence is to the victim or his survivors. PNoy's legal team is quiet and should not protest too much. Or at all.

But, graft, filed by gutsy Ombudsman Chit Morales, is something else. One charged with it, as PNoy is, in effect is being labelled a crook. No probation necessarily available on conviction for a grafter. Bad faith is involved. Evil and malice mark the offense.

The Mamasapano operation resulted in terrorist Marwan being sent to the Muslim paradise where virgins await deflowering by a martyr.

Casualties? One should remain a civilian or avoid

being sent to fight historically fierce Muslim warriors to avoid the risks that go with joining special operation forces against them. Lore has it that Black Jack Pershing had the lethal .45 pistol devised to stop fanatical Muslim juramentados. Howling dervishes, sort of.

And it should be Mamasapano 62 to include the Muslim victims. Their lives also mattered. Not to forget that the goal of bagging Marwan by those singing "ang mamatay nang dahil sa 'yo" was attained. So, not a total failure unlike Jack Kennedy' s Bay of Pigs and Bill Clinton' s Blackhawk Down debacles. Neither was charged for failure. And rightly so. They answered to their conscience, and to history. "La historia me absolvera," cried Fidel Castro. "History will absolve me." They were not asked to pay the families of heroes or victims of collateral damage for judgment calls in good faith. If there is financial assistance, well and good, but heroism is not necessarily monetized.

The Constitution cannot and does not require a Prez to be perfect or infallible. To err is human. And here, PNoy was not in noncompliance with any statute in our scofflaw nation. Washington enlisted the aid of chemist Sean Connery, a convict, in the movie, The Rock. In the film Dirty Dozen, the convicted murderous maniacs (e.g., Charles Bronson, death by hanging, Digong's weapon of choice, as it were) became heroes. And former

Top Cop Alan Purisima is only an accused, charged with PNoy. Not even a convict.

Charged reportedly with violating Sec. 7 of R.A. No. 3019 (1960) and Sec. 8 of R.A. No. 6713 (1989), is Chief Justice Meilou Sereno; everyone in

government from Prez Digong down to the last barangay dogcatcher may have a problem. Said Sec. 7 mandates filing by a public servant, of "a statement of the amounts and sources of his income, the amounts of his personal and family expenses and the amount of income taxes paid for the next preceding calendar year." Its Sec. 2(b) defines a"public officer" as including "elective and appointive officials and employees, permanent or temporary, whether in the classified or unclassified or exemption service receiving compensation, even nominal, from the government. . . ."

If the House, busy with impeachment, looks at compliance with Sec. 7, its members should be prepared to show their own filings thereunder.   If the Prez or his Cabinet members, or any one else for that matter, can show compliance with Sec. 7 last year, I'll eat it.

This provision may cover the fascinating consultative body the Prez created last week. Misogynistic, I submit, for naming only one woman out of 19 (thus far). From where I sit, she may be a household word only in her own household, with all due respect. Ka Celing Muñoz-Palma she isn't; no wonder she is named Ms. Susan-Hubalde Ordinario, maybe to stress that Digong much cares for ordinary folk. There are six more vacancies so there is time to heed the saying that the best man for the job is a woman, to join Ms. Susan, who I wish Godspeed (the name of co-star Nicholas Cage, in The Rock).

The body of consultants will meet for a year, derailing and shooting down Speaker Bebot's reported choo-choo bullet train arrival date of May 2018. Its members must be preparing now to comply with Sec. 7 of R.A. No. 3019 which requires one to file the required statement within a month "after assuming office." We need to know where its office will be, whether the members can hire staff, etc.. Indeed, paging DBM Sec. Ben Diokno: how much will the consultancy cost the taxpayer? I bet he cannot find a single tree with money growing on it. The Constitutional Consultants, comprising an ad hoc body, will work for about a year.

Our present Consti has a State Policy against dynasties. Yet, we saw a Prez Duterte, Mayor Duterte and Vice Mayor Duterte. I seem to be the only one to grouse about it. Maybe others do but of which I am not aware. All seem to be afraid of the Godfather (I pretend not to be). The foreign model we now have seems to have originated in Sicily.

Basically, the problem has been one of implementation of our laws. A scofflaw nation we have been since Macoy - Digong's idol - took over in the 60's and opened his William Saunders' account in Switzerland while Imelda opened her Jane Ryan's. Money for The Restoration?

Will a new Constitution make a difference?

Yup, Rappler' s mortal sin is that it has not behaved like Mocha Uson, who venerates the Godfather, who commends Aung San Suu Kyi on Rohingya, urging her to ignore us, useless human rights critics and advocates.

I have ageing-ailing issues. And I don't know what type of federalism we may get into. What I now seem to see arguably can be traced to Sicily, with a fellow Bedan for a Godfather (Duterte), capo di tutti capi, boss of all bosses, aided and abetted by Bedan Consigliere (Medialdea and Aguirre). And enforcers like Bato de la Rosa implementing a population

reduction program. Another Bedan is gutsy Leila de Lima, our own Dolores Ibarruri, La Pasionaria.

At this point lawyers, led by the IBP, I for Inspiring - OK, Integrated Bar of the Philippines) , cannot do more than warn fervently against a Balkanizing federalism which may lead us to become Somalia or Venezuela, basket cases. At some point, lawyers may file cases but per se any chacha effort cannot be enjoined. More speech, not less. The noises and sounds of democracy.

Gising! Bangon! Manindigan! Shakespeare wrote, "first thing we do, let's kill all the lawyers," in praise, not dispraise, of the profession. They ask the foolish questions of the day, as Tañada, Diokno, Salonga, Arroyo, et al. did, when Digong's idol ruled and reigned and ruined our values, processes and institutions from which we have yet to recover. If we ever will, . . . enslaved as we have been for centuries.

"When will [we] ever learn? Long time passing. . . ."

The Catholic Bishops, who have played key roles in changes in the past, have warned against a "creeping dictatorship, " which some see   even now as "galloping. "

I am more concerned about "political syndicalism, " as it were.

oooooo

19

Revgov? Impeachment Blues

Nov. 23, 2017,

Chief Justice (CJ) Art Panganiban, in his typically edifying November 19, 2017 column, along with many other constitutional scholars, seems to assume casually that the removal of Marcos in 1986, was not in accord with the 1973 Constitution.

The 1973 Constitution I call Siopao; the barangays were said to have been convened, and asked who wanted Siopao - almost all attendees raised their hands. The Comelec tallied the raised hands as "Yes." I wasn't aware though of any such Assembly being held in the places I was familiar with. In any event, our Constitutions of 1935 (Art. VII, Sec. 9), 1973 (Art. VII, Sec. 9) and 1987 (Art. VII, Sec. 8) all say that a President's term may be ended by "removal from office."

The People "removed" Marcos in 1986, to local and world acclaim. Erap was "removed" in 2001, at which the world, puzzled, looked askance, but which "removal" arguably, was not unconstitutional, on the basis of the constitutional language. However, the Supreme Court (SC) instead ruled that he had resigned, on the weird basis of somebody else's diary. Baffling to the outside world and to certain of us, natives. But, "removal" could have led to a Revolutionary Government (RevGov) and the wise Justices may find themselves jobless, as in 1986. Hence, resignation, as one theory.

Erap's lawyers (I wasn't one of them yet) had prudently advised that he write to the Senate Prez and the Speaker that he was stepping ASIDE due to temporary disability, not stepping DOWN. He did so and was the last one to know he had resigned kuno.

Out of power, overdog-turned-underdog Erap renewed his invite that I join his legal team. I did. When I orally argued the case in the Supreme
Court, there was no discussion I could recall on resignation. But, if a Justice had raised the issue of whether he was "removed" by some people and the military, in the same way we removed Marcos, I might have had "little" wiggle room. But, the Justices might have realized that their own tenure might be in jeopardy.

We need a law on the procedure on resignations, to clarify such issues as to who

Comelec Chair Andy Bautista should have submitted his resignation. In the U.S., Nixon submitted his letter to the Secretary of State, as explicitly provided by 3 U.S Code Sec. 20.

My attempts to have such a local clarifying law did not get anywhere in the 1987-92 Senate. It's time someone in the legislature should start the process of filling up the lacuna. But, it seems the lawmakers would rather probe in aid of something and impeach, also in aid of something and I fret about the way Congress expects a guest to check the Bill of Rights at the door. It is said that a lawyer who defends himself has a fool for a client, as the House well knows, which it should factor in. (And, do the solons and others have to eat in the session hall? *Ten am pa lang the other day. . . .*) Impeachment may lead to the capital penalty of removal and the target should be given every leeway. Sporting and fair was what guided a House panel in the impeachment of Federal Judge Alcee L. Hastings."It granted the defense" the extraordinary prerogative of his counsel [Terence J. Anderson] to question any of the witnesses, if he so chooses, for up to the point of 10 minutes" . Impeachment Inquiry, Hearings, Subcommittee on Criminal Justice, Pursuant to H. Res. 128, Impeaching AlceeL. Hastings, May 18, 1988, Serial No. 11, p. 8.

In my first year or so of practice, cross-examination was allowed in preliminary investigations. In one case, Manila Fiscal Serafin Cuevas allowed us, as counsel, to cross-examine. I learned a lot watching famed iconic soft-spoken Doy Quisumbing cross. Marcos removed that right, facilitating the prosecution of "subversives." Impeachment is sui generis, in a class by itself, and the House should consider allowing it, to mitigate its image as an extension of Malacañang.

CJ Meilou's basic offense, from where I sit, is asserting judicial independence, which may get in the way of a RevGov. Like Senator Leila de Lima, had she kept quiet or voted the way Digong was seen to favor, she would "most likely" not be undergoing her current ordeal. Another offense: she was seen to jump the queue - from a relatively junior Associate, to Chief - and generated sadness. (I supported another aspirant in 2012 but support her now as one legitimate CJ, which was more than I "regret to have to say for post midnight-appointee Rene Corona.)"

If her lawyers file a case in the SC, she would have to inhibit herself but it would also smoke out her fellow magistrates into recusing themselves if they would be witnesses against her, as ballyhooed.

Seniority may be sacred here but it is nothing in the U.S. Supreme Court. CJ Roberts was not even an Associate Justice when elevated. No resentment from those bypassed who may have had an understandable moist eye cast on the Chief Justiceship. (In January 1987, turned down a signed SC appointment; public service its its own reward, my mantra, and I, then 47, saw many far more deserving seniors. Non sibi sed patriae; not self, but country) Anyway, Holmes and J.B.L. Reyes, et al., are better remembered fondly than CJs, like Roger Taney, a Catholic who ruled that blacks were chattels in the 1857 Dred Scott case.

Congress is better off lawmaking and policymaking, not probing and impeaching and judging. Lavish lifestyle for getting an expensive car for court use? Eventually, all 15 should get one, state-of-the- art; on SALN, punished lightly in R.A. No. 6713, has she been given a chance to amplify or correct, if needed? CJ telling Judges not to surrender without a warrant, which document

the Constitution requires? Of course it is said that impeachment is political but not to the point of making it a Kenkoy proceeding. We need to study harder the history of impeachment of magistrates in the U.S., England and even India. Only U.S. S.C. Justice Samuel Chase was impeached; impeachment failed. Chase acquitted.

ASEAN was not a failure. No occasion to blurt out, Putin Ina! Xia-pao Naman! Trumpong Kangkarot! (Our Rizal High "Rizalian" graduation issue labelled me Galawgaw.) But, its effect on traffic is something to note. No gridlocks then, which we again have, and how! This is what Digong may properly apologize for, not the MRT glitches about which he could have done nothing. Wotta lucky guy. In the San Beda-Lyceum face-off last week, as an alum of both schools, no way Digong could have lost.

Sec. Art Tugade was in Araneta and maybe chanted with us Umpa! Umpa! Beda-Beda-Beda- Fight, etc., which never fails to whip Bedan blood).

But, easy on Digong's use of addictive pain-killer Fentanyl. The Nov. 20, 2017 issue of TIME said: "[I]n 2016, the Drug Enforcement Administration (DEA) reported more than 30,000 seizures of fentanyl, a dramatic spike from the 5,000 documented in 2014. The man-made formulas are so powerful that police officers participating in drug raids where fentanyl is confiscated have overdosed simply by breathing in particles of the drug released into the air. . . . The opioid epidemic may have been sparked by prescription medications, but it's now a label for a much larger addiction crisis in the U.S., spanning dozens of drugs both legal and not." At 36-37. An old problem. Macoy's mother was arrested, suspected to have sold opium and heroin to Arellano Hi students, according to Tibo Mijares in Conjugal Dictatorship. The Marcoses were that poor then.*

Addiction and overdose may kill one but the state does not rush death in the U.S. by EJKs. "You' re killing yourself by addiction, the PNP will do you a favor by EJKs," seems to be the mantra here, reducing our population by thousands. We should share the pain of addicts and their loved ones. We wish the Philippine Drug Enforcement Agency luck. Reduce population by Kill-Kill-Kill not its style.

In limiting our population, only two kids suggested but how about only one wife (and perhaps one kulasisi for each macho)? Who are our role models? Ideally, only one wife, but if kulasisis are factored in, nothing doing. Digong has a fave partner on public occasions he should marry so as not to confuse the youth, prosecutors and judges. He is reported to have kulasisis in Davao and Cagayan de Oro, per scuttlebutt. Speaker Bebot Alvarez converted to a tribe in Mindanao allowing more than one wife and famously asked who among us has no kulasisi? Are we really a nation of Lady-Killers?

I label Lady-Killers as emotional terrorists even as we label the NPAs as terrorists, but we may not properly take into account why the latter rebel. They may be citizens with a grievance, e.g., a farmer whose daughter gets raped by an hacendero, who is not prosecuted or if prosecuted, gets acquitted. The farmer may then go out of the system.

But, what is Prez Digong's excuse for going RevGov? May we have a Heal-Heal-Heal, not Kill-Kill-Kill, presidency instead?

So my mantra, the right thing must be done in the right way at the right time in the right place for the right reason. Thus - "The key to successful extramarital sex, therefore, was discretion. Mrs. Patrick Campbell, perhaps the most outspoken woman in polite Victorian society, said dryly: `It doesn't matter what you do in the bedroom, as long as you don't do it in the street and frighten the horses'. "W. Manchester, The Last Lion - Winston Spencer Churchill 74 (1974, paperback)." Here, discretion not needed, per Speaker Bebot Alvarez. Wide-open society. In decay.(?)

Digong must keep my five R's Mantra in mind. Be careful with RevGov, and maybe, faithful Honeylet deserves matrimony. Talking about Leila's guilt is improper. I am again reminded of her because Charles Manson just died at 83. Nixon blasted him as guilty of the rape-murder of pregnant Sharon Tate, and the killing of others. The public howled. The White House was quick to apologize; no, it did not mean to prejudge.

Have Digong, Sec. Vit Aguirre (another one now with a moist eye cast on the Senate) and SolGen Joe Calida talked too much about Leila's supposed guilt? Had she kept quiet, she would now be in the Senate where, with any kind of luck - I never underrate anyone's capacity for subjective growth - we may have Prez Manny Pacquiao (now bored in the Senate) shine and and go for the whole enchilada, with Veep Mocha Uson in 2022. Those concerned may all play coy but if ordered to run by Digong, who are they to say no?

Play coy, I urge, and not to say China is "privileged; to be third telcos player. Let it compete and bid. Else, if unbidden, it comes, we may feel like the Pop, who, asked for her daughter' s hand, had to say, "sure, you might as well have her hand. You have had everything else." *Pakipot muna. Hele-hele, bago quiere.*

And charge, not just shame Gen. Dionisio Santiago, so he can defend himself in some proper forum. Same fate as Sec. Mike Sueno's. The Palace convicted and shamed them without due process.

Palace, I don't like your style.

oooooo

20

Lack of Inter-Branch Courtesy; Answering to History

Nov 8, 2017,

As spokesperson of then candidate Cory Aquino in 1985-86, it was a pleasant task for me to announce that Manang Letty Ramos-Shahani, then in the foreign service, had come out openly in support of our candidate, in defiance of the dictator. Then came the equally public and bold defection

of Col. Mariano Santiago, a hero in Edsa'86. I was reminded of him because his brother, General Dionisio had just resigned/retired or fired as PDEA

chief. Running in the family is high principle, at stake in a pending impeachment proceeding.

I endorsed another candidate for Chief Justice (CJ) in 2012, not Associate Justice Meilou Sereno. But, the President' s call was for her, which was legit and totally in order. So unlike the gross post-midnight appointment of her predecessor, which called for institutional correction, by the people, thru their Representatives, done via impeachment, and by their Senators, via conviction and removal.

Now, courtesy seems to be in very short supply in this mal-administration. *So bastos! La cortesia no quita la valentia,* the Palace should remember. Courtesy does not detract from valor.

Every Justice, among many many others, has his moist eye cast on the Chief Justiceship, so I can understand the seeming lack of intramural

support. But, it is not only the institution but the country itself at stake.

I am incredulous at the rate Harry Roque arguably appears to be self-destructing. For him, and not say, remarkable Sal Panelo, to say CJ Meilou must resign so as not to damage the Supreme Court, sounds bizarre. What about the damage to the country' s institutional arrangements by such egregious lack of inter-departmental courtesy?

So, here's another stone, from where I sit, but I rightly don't know whether Harry will go to a hollow block factory or a bakery. Santa banana! Not satisfied with speaking for the Philippines, he now seems to speak also for China and its intentions. By what authority naman kaya? If he can really speak for China, he might find some way for it to stop exporting shabu to the Philippines. We watch what others do, not what they say. Does China really insist on using its labor force in its infrastructure projects here with our high unemployment? While making us stop doing what we want in our very own?

Even more, or equally, startling is UP Manila's opposition to medical marijuana, echoing the Philippine Medical Association. They may assume that the U.S., Canada, and many countries in South America and Europe are insane not to oppose marijuana. Bill Clinton, Dubya Bush and Barack Obama all flirted with Mary Jane, which may explain why Bill, as sexual predator, later romanced Moooannniiicccaa Lewinsky.

What an individual does to destroy himself, with marijuana, the state would take over, by imprisoning, in some stinking overcrowded jail, and
stigmatizing, a user, for life or a loooong time.

Portugal has decriminalized all drugs and sees users as sick frail people to be saved and rehabbed, not criminals to be destroyed by a prison
record. But, things seem normal enough there. After an initial spike in use 15 or so years ago, it went down. And I have friends who went to Fatima last month, to mark the centennial of our Lady's Apparition in Portugal. Antonio Guterres is the new SecGen of the UN, where its General Assembly
Special Session on drugs is moving towards liberalization.

Our Catholic Church supports medical marijuana use to deal with suffering.

Decriminalizing should kill the syndicates because the state will supply for free, or at nominal cost, in rehab facilities what syndicates charge in humongous sums. Kill the profit motive and kill trafficking.

China can prove its friendship by knocking off its shabu supply source. A small price to pay for our virtual dishonorable surrender of West Philippine Sea.

Last Tuesday, San Sebastian surrendered honorably to San Beda. I got to watch the game

for all the NCAA semifinal marbles at the Mall of Asia
Arena. Initially, I was seated at the Baste side. I had on a yellow shirt (Baste's color) and a red jacket**** (San Beda's). Then I was moved to courtside.

San Beda outlasted San Sebastian, which fought gallantly, and the Lions will now face the Lyceum juggernaut.

I missed our Indian Yell that whips the blood and our former rousing Victory Song. I still feel antsy as to why the losers are made to stay on court and sing. They should be allowed to go at once to their locker room, and let alone to weep, in privacy.

Attendance was all right last Tuesday but the title series which begins today, in Araneta, another planet which is farther, and I cannot go to, I fear. I live in Palanan and the other night, for a meeting in Conti's in Greenbelt, nearly two hours it took me. This is where the administration&# 39;s Kill-Pa-More policy may be needed, which seems to be overdoing it in the messy bloody and failed drug war.

Take-Prisoners- for-Rehab will do.

No incident, much less a rhubarb or donnybrook, marred last Tuesday' s NCAA offering. Commissioner Bai Cristobal and the three refs deserve kudos. Two years ago, when San Beda lost to Letran, 82-85, in overtime. in the final game, the Three Blind Mice didn't see a lane violation with seconds to go. But, that's all right. San Beda owes it to one and all to remind them from time to time that it is not the only team in the league.

And Robert Bolick, like Jerry West in the 1970 NBA Finals, made an even longer shot from the foul line, a buzzer-beater, last Tuesday; without it, the score would have been a close 73-71. More than worth the price of admission. (OK, I had a free ducat.)

Looming is another Thrilla.

PNoy is charged in the Sandiganbayan for Mamasapano, an operation that bagged Marwan, who had at least $5M on his head. No one runs for Prez claiming perfection and infallibility. Else, only the likes of Bedan Justice Gregorio Perfecto would qualify. When troopers go to enemy lair, particularly Morolandia, they knew some would come back in boxes.

Kennedy and the Bay of Pigs, Johnson and the Tet Offensive, Carter and the Iran rescue, Reagan and the Marines in Beirut, the Bushes and Obama in Iraq, and Clinton in Black Hawk Down, might have erred and misjudged, but with no personal gain. To err is human.

And like Fidel Castro, proclaim, "la historia me absolvera!" ** History will absolve me, PNoy can say. Indeed, the like the American Presidents,   he should not have even been charged.

There is no talk even of going after those who killed comrades in fatal friendly fire in Marawi. Nor of why Digong was in Russia when the   Marawi bloodletting began. And rightly so even if military intelligence again surfaced as a seeming contradiction in terms. *Sino po ang mga natulog*

sa
pansitan, resulting in having to destroy Marawi in order to save it? Like Vietnam' s Ben Tre?

Graft in PNoy's situation is hard to fathom. Usurpation? What, pray tell, is a Prez and Commander-in- Chief, prohibited from doing within his executive domain?

Saguisag & Associates Lawyers 4045 Bigasan Street, Palanan 1235 Makati Office Nos. (+632) 551-6350/833-4140 Fax No. (+632) 831-2276

oooooo

21

When Harry Met Rody

Nov. 1, 2017

Our newspapers should have someone like Linda Greenhouse of the New York Times, when reporting or commenting on an item with a legal dimension.

Too often, local media for instance mis-report a motion for reconsideration (before the same court) as an appeal (to a higher court.)

Even legal thriller novelist John Grisham, a lawyer who writes so well, might need a tighter editor. I have enjoyed in particular his novels with a sports angle, such as Calico Joe (baseball, 2012) and Playing for Pizza (American pro football, 2007). I was incredulous to see John seemingly commit what we here often do: "The fact that [quarterback] Rick was now a fugitive added a level of daring and romance that the Italians found irresistible. In a country where laws are flaunted and those who flaunt them are often glamorized, the pursuit by the police was the dominant topic whenever two or more [Parma] Panthers got together." At 221, paperback. It seems to me "flaunted", often misused here, should be "flouted". But, who am I to correct a native English speaker who writes so well?*

"Subornation of perjury" is to induce to perjure. But, a statement attributed to a Supreme Court Justice' s staff supposedly stated "subordination or perjury." Phil. Star, Oct. 27, 2017, p. 2, col. 4. *Susmariano po naman! Typo po malamang*. I am incredulous that such a high-level staff would commit such an egregious lapse.

A newspaper' s copy reader or ombudsman should also ban any further misstatement that Ferdinand E. Marcos was born on September 11, 1917. It should be 1916. I have a copy of his birth certificate, affirming what he said under oath in a Honolulu court in 1986, as I recall it. Kim Lumagbas, a San Beda Alabang Law stude of mine produced Macoy's birth certificate, echoed by seven others. ABS-CBN should get part of the credit for publishing that fact in 1998, thanks to Melvin dela Cuesta. Indeed, if anyone can show me a Macoy birth certificate carrying 1917, I will eat it.

The Philippine Postal Corporation has to be probed by the Ombudsman, Department of Justice and the Commission on Audit for falsifying history and wasting government funds on a commemorative stamp for the kleptocrat/human rights violator. 2017 is not his centennial, but his 101st birth anniversary. Next time I visit the burial ground of my late father-in-law in Libingan ng Mga Bayani, I just may consider trying to go visit Apo's resting place and see if the epitaph says: HERE A LAWYER LIES STILL, found in an Irish cemetery.

The destruction of our values, institutions and processes Macoy accelerated in the 60's-80's, following World War II, when we still had vestiges of old-fashioned delicadeza and palabra de honor, which ruination continues full blast today. Let's hope new presidential spokesperson Harry Roque will demonstrate a better command of language than Meyor/Prez Rody himself, Martin Andanar and Sal Panelo, with their rather constipated vocabulary. Thus, the regrettable resort to kabastusan. Too bad urbane Ernesto Abella had to be let go. No room for the non-lawyer's urbanidad. Now, a Digong, Jr., sa kahambugan? But, I hope Harry regards me as a friend; recall Napoleon advising not to disrupt an enemy making a mistake.

I was candidate, Prez-elect and Prez Cory's echo and I would tell the Palace Brat Pack, "that is what I was told to say, I am not allowed to think here, puede ba, next question," and we'd would move on. Brilliant creative Teddy Boy Locsin, another presidential echo, was on his own when he made the inelegant "You' re No. 1" gesture with his right middle finger. Muy pillo.

Cory had breeding and elegance, previously required or expected of our officials, particularly high ones. (I made her lose her temper only once, when I remarked early

December 1989, at the height of a coup, that Senate Prez Salonga was right: there was a perception of her double captivity, by the military and the U.S.; when I got home, my wife at once barked, "ano yung itinawag ni Cory that between her and Uncle Jovy, atbp."; double captivity I was in, by two women I cherished.) Mar Roxas got it when

once he used "PI!" That Digong is not getting it for far cruder lingo galore suggests we may be decaying faster than seems possible. The Cycle is Savagery, Civilization and Decay.

Sticks and stones may break my bones but words can never hurt me? But, words can hurt too, and the new presidential mouthpiece is shopping for hollow blocks, to throw at us, making us cower in fear. We are cowards pretending not to be so.

If a farmer, after failing to get justice for a daughter raped by an hacendero, throws a stone at the system, I am incredulous that Harry says to throw a hollow block at the peasant. Many who join the NPA are poor, with unredressed grievances, as the law too often represents the biases of the ruling classes. I am glad that mercurial Digong could sound more conciliatory, last we heard.

A Senator was quoted here last Sunday to say "senators won't allow suspects to invoke their right to against self-incrimination without a valid reason." Our Constitution does not work in the Senate? "Valid reason" enough for me, the human and constitutional right not to speak. It seems   to me suspects can just cite the Bill of Rights

(Artikulo III, name of our new lawyers' group). Most any lawyer's first advice to any suspect is to "shut
up," which the Constitution protects, while the attorney tries to build the strongest possible defense under the laws of the land.

To entice a suspect to talk, not to his own perdition, he should be offered effective immunity which only a court, I believe, can grant. The legislative Committee on a proper vote should go to some court which would cooperate as a co-worker in government, the U.S. praxis. Congress cannot
usurp a judicial function in exempting one from prosecution.

Yes, where in the Constitution is Congress given the power to detain because someone is not aiding it in doing its job - legislation? What law does the Senate have in mind that they now need the aid of harassed terrorized and bullied laymen anyway? Intimidation and terrorism our public servants should shy away from. Forgetting purposes is the most common form of innocence, to paraphrase Nietzsche. Guests or resource persons should never be identified by the Senate as "suspects" ;, more proper in a police stationhouse, where the mantra begins with, "you have a right to remain silent, . . ."?

The Justice Secretary should not usurp the judicial function of a court in granting immunity, either. He can only ask some court, not impose on it, per Sec. 7 of Rule 119 of the Rules of Court.

Lawmakers and Cabinet Members should study, instead of joining us in having to spend too much time in traffic, taking pixes/selfies and watching basketball games where we cannot be world-class and have to import players and even coaches. *Josme po naman*. What time is left for productive effort seen in the progressive countries?

This is 2017, not the middle ages or the period of cruel Inquisition. Lawmakers should legislate for our people, and not flagellate, guests.

For instance, last week an "exclusive club" admitted me (with two others). When I asked for the check, I saw it was for P1,800.00. I tendered P2,000.00, in cash. It was rejected, along with my senior citizen' s card (and only a credit card would do). Paging Romy Macalintal. Is remedial legislation needed on what is meant by "legal tender" in exclusive plutocratic enclaves where I obviously don't belong? Congress should study my plaint.

Romy and I wish our pal, Harry Roque, well, in the bowels of labyrinthine serpentine Malacañang. We count on him having a broader vocabulary than what Digong Duterte, Sal Panelo and Mart Andanar have shown so far. Harry should say whoa, whoa to our *napakadaldal na Pangulo. Be real, not plastic. Huwag magtaksil sa kanyang kauri.*

I am reminded of the film When Harry Met Sally; there, Meg Ryan moaned and faked an orgasm in a resto, prompting another woman to tell the waiter she wanted whatever Meg had ordered. (There was a town known as Sexmoan in Pampanga, now Sasmuan).

Teka, teka, this is a family newspaper nga pala. Our family's Undas is on the 8th, next week, when I mark a decade of my being an Unmerry

Widower. No gridlock, or less, by then, when we will troop to Manila Memorial. I believe it was Gen. Mon Farolan who more than once wisely suggested that we go on birth or death anniversaries, instead of overcrowding on November 1.

Tradition? As I recall reading in Selecciones de Reader's Digest decades ago, a tradition is a social vice that has become incurable (*la tradicion es un vicio social que se ha vuelto incurable*). Undas in my youth in Pasig we associated with stealing chickens. Now, larceny could be for purloining P50M, less a thou, for bailable graft, instead of non-bailable plunder, for Digong's frat brods. But, of course innocence is presumed, save apparently in Congress and Malaca¤ang, the graveyard of the Bill of Rights for critics, who should now ready themselves for Harry's hollow blocks.

What a hollow blockhead Halloween idea for governance. But, I support Digong on the Balangiga Bells. Also, on the Bangsamoro Basic Law, and here Senator Leila joins us. Kudos, Lei, for deserving the "Prize for Freedom" , a feat you share with Prez Cory, who told me in December 1989, "from now on, things won't be hunky-dory," and proceeded to make sumbong to my ever-loving Dulce.

See you on the 8th, my luv.

ooooo

22

LIVES WELL LIVED; LEILA'S MISTRIAL

Oct 18, 2017

San Beda Class'63 law class. Last Saturday, the Bulletin carried a prominent obit (not vying of course with the venerable Wash Sycip's many deserved tributes) on his "homegoing last Saturday. Condolences.

I saw the Archie obit when I was in a hurry to go to my Saturday classes. Barely made it in Mendiola and late in Alabang. Traffic. Worse than ever, after Digong took power, and therefore, responsibility.

But, why worry? Why hurry? Golf pro Walter Hagen advised not to do either, for we are here only for a short visit, so why not stop and smell the flowers? - he asked, rhetorically (popularized by John Dean in the Watergate scandal). Indeed, what is the meaning of life? Whose life is not being well-lived?

Inquirer columnist Mon Tulfo, a Digong supporter (who I saw in QC the other afternoon), I agree with, when he, in effect said the Prez needs to stop and smell the flowers. Note that on Andy Bautista' s situation or resignation, what Digong supposedly said last Saturday, disturbed: "Nagtaka ako, it was the other day, he [filed his] resignation. Mukhang pinirmahan ko." Mon is right. "Mukhang pinirmahan ko"? Digong needs a vacation so he will know and remember what he is doing, and saying. At 72, he cannot be senile yet. (But, I can be, at 78, in my second childhood; Digong is into his second adolescence, with what he shares with Mon, RH, for Raging Hormones. Two Kamandags. But, really, has Andy submitted his resignation to the proper party? We need a law on resignations.

I filed a bill on the matter in my time in the Senate, only to lie and die there.

Like father, like daughter. Tough Davao City Mayor Sara mentions Senator Sonny Trillanes's "balls." Were they subjected to autoptic proference or ocular inspection I would not be surprised if Sonny has at least three, judging by his fearless "fiscalizing&q uot; - in quotes as no dictionary I have looked at seems to carry this Filipinism - of a very popular populist Prez.

On the Duterte assets, it seems to me a good way, maybe the best way, is to execute a bank secrecy waiver, instead of dissembling. But maybe, just maybe, the lawyers of CJ Meilou Sereno are right, the Statement of Assets, etc. (or SALNs) contains the waiver. Arguable because the Salonga Law (R.A. No. 6713, which shafted a Chief Justice (Rene Corona), and which I had sponsored on the floor, says, in its Sec. 8 (A): "All public official and employees required to file [SALNs] shall also execute within thirty (30) from the date of their assumption of office, the necessary authority in favor of the Ombudsman to obtain from all appropriate government agencies, including the Bureau of Internal Revenue, such documents as may show their liabilities, net worth, and also their business interests and financial connections in previous years, including, if possible the year when they first assumed any office in the government."

But, private banks are not "government agencies," so the need for a bank waiver in the case of the Dutertes, who may or may not have executed such "authority. " Indeed, who among our 1,600,000 public servants in this scofflaw nation have?

If CJ Meilou is not getting open support from the judiciary, it may be because of understandable self-interest, to avoid nightmarish prosecution/ persecution by our fightingest Prez and/or enhance moving-up dreams.

It may be the Dutertes are living in their alternative universe in asking Sonny to prove his allegations that they have accounts in Davao and Ortigas, information best known to them; veiled by legal secrecy, sans waivers. The burden shifts when the matter is best known to a party. The Dutertes can just waive their right to secrecy to shatter into smithereens Sonny's claim that Vice Mayor Pulong has more than a hundred million pesos in a Davao bank while Digong has billions in a BPI bank in Ortigas. In the process, destroy Sonny. Bakit po pakendeng-kendeng pa?

Presidential Legal Counsel Sal Panelo says the allegations are based on just rumors. Precisely, all the more, what better way to show their being so by having the banks show the paper trails.

If Sonny's allegations are false, the Dutertes can sue Sonny for defamation, who, in his defense can however have the bank records subpoenaed, finally. If he is charged and convicted in a libel case, there may or may not be jail time but Sonny can be crippled by humongous sums of damages extracted from him. His public life may also come to an end if the record establishes recklessness.

1,600,000 waivers by public servants. Senator Gatchalian may be one of them; but as Master, he now recklessly threatens to cite a fratman in contempt as reported here last Sunday. He reportedly said petulantly, "nakakainit ng ulo itong luko-loko [John Paul Solano] na ito." What gives the servant the right to insult a master, the citizen, a particle of popular sovereignty, so casually? What does such cavalier pose tell the young?

A cop would need to say "you have a right to remain silent, . . ." Therefore immunity must be granted a guest which in the U.S. only a court may grant to the snitch. No Bill of Rights in our Senate? Congress is the NBI-PNP writ large which does not start with "you have a right to remain silent," but bamboozles or terrorized guests to sing like canaries.

Talagang bastusan na. Digong said Leila is a "prisoner of her lust," reacting to her assertion that she is a "prisoner of conscience." Leila deserves to be jailed, per Digong, commenting on a case which is sub judice, which concept no one seems to honor hereabouts. But, he should be above the fray. He has many attack dogs.

When Nixon said on August 3, 1970, that Charles Manson was guilty, the White House scrambled to explain and apologize, in that Nixon failed to use "alleged" and did not mean to prejudge the case - to deal with the firestorm of criticism. Here, the Prez regularly prejudges Leila and would never say what Nixon did, who said he was "misunderstood ." - "The last thing I would do is prejudice the legal rights of any person, in any circumstances. To set the record straight, I do not now and did not intend to speculate whether the [actress Sharon] Tate defendants are guilty, in fact or not. All the facts in the case have not yet been presented. The defendants should be presumed to be innocent at this stage of the trial."

Many opined "that if Manson was convicted, the conviction would be reversed on appeal because of Nixon's statement."

"[T]he next day [Aug. 4, three female accused] stood up and said in perfect unison: `Your Honor, the President said we are guilty, so why go on with the trial?" V. Bugliosi, Helter Skelter 438-39, 444 (1974).

The case against Leila should be dismissed on the ground of mistrial to educate one and all. In a police custodial interrogation, the prober starts with "you have a right to remain silent, etc." Why should the Bill of Rights, intact in a police stationhouse, be checked at the door of the Palace or of Congress? A frat man is threatened with contempt for not talking via an affidavit.

The Senate is not the PNP-NBI writ large. In the U.S., any guest can cite the Fifth, i.e., the right to remain silent. The U.S. Congress cannot grant immunity. It has to go to court to get it, which is routinely obtained. Only then may the guest be forced to speak.

Nowhere in the Constitution is Congress granted the right to detain one who exercises his right not to speak. The Inquisition ended centuries ago elsewhere, but continues here? Only an effectively immunized guest can be coerced to speak.

Last Sunday, this paper reported: "`America knows': Drug charges filed against de Lima `real.' - Duterte." Our quarrelsome madaldal Prez should not talk on the guilt of any person, as all decision-makers want to be safe from his wrath or desirous of promotion. No one seems to observe the sub judice rule, of not talking on the guilt of anyone in a pending case (and the Supreme Court shamelessly leaks like a sieve, to the benefit of our enterprising Jomar Canlas, the 16th Justice). If I say an accused is innocent, I just repeat the presumption of innocence.

Digong keeps convicting and disparaging Leila. This is for rottweiler Sal Panelo, not he, to say, if at all. Not presidential, and violates the Bill of Rights. Artikulo III, our new human rights aggrupation, another Filipinism in a country where some pronounced awry as au-ree and not as aray, and chaos as tsaos, and not as kay-os).

So, Digong, don't hurry, don't worry, stop and smell the flowers. And please stop misusing the human rights salute by raising a clenched fist. No need to taunt fallen enemy commanders/combatants. The Marawi victory reminds me of what was said of Ben Tre in Viet Nam, that the village was destroyed in order to save it, by Pulitzer Prize winner Peter Arnett, quoting an unnamed army officer.

And avoid wishful thinking like the UN taking over a failed bloody, messy drug war that has not succeeded anywhere. Its new SecGen, Antonio Guterres, is from Portugal, which decriminalized all drugs more than 15 years ago. It has not been destroyed. Indeed, some ballroom mates of mine have gone there for the Fatima Centennial this month. Prayers are what we need more of. Too bad Ricardo Cardinal Vidal, another hero of 1986 in ousting Macoy, is gone.

oooooo

23

WHAT I'VE LEARNED

Oct. 6, 2017 – rewrite (archive 1987)

(This was emailed to me by my friend Camilo Abogado, dated Oct. 6, 2017, with article by Rene Saguisag, good man indeed... needed for a bad times like this....I adopt saguisag in 1987. in 1987 senatorial election,some voters think that Rene Saguisag's name is Adopt.. :-D

I'm lucky to be accepted as volunteers of Saguisag.. we would campaign for him in Camanava Area, the slums of Malabon, Navotas and Caloocan, we eat in every palengke's carinderia in the area. we also campaign for him in Cavite area... yanother exciting experience where we would see armed persons roaming in the campaign area, an exciting experience for enthusiastic youth like us. we have no salary, no allowance. a true sundalong kanin...we are free lunch volunteers; those are good deeds done for good man like Saguisag..those are best times we have to help a person with human rights advocacy.... and we never got disappointed..)

WHAT I'VE LEARNED
Rene Saguisag, ESQUIRE PHILIPPINES

When I left for the US [to study law], maybe I was 100 miles to the right of Marcos. I didn't like students telling the leaders how to run the country. I was very conservative. But in '67 when I got in, that was the height of the Vietnam protest. At times, it was very hard to go to Harvard because of the demonstrations. And then the following year, I went to Berkeley, another hotbed, there would be tear gas. That was part of my education in the US. Martin Luther King was assassinated, Bobby Kennedy was assassinated … those developments could not have left me unaffected. And when I came home (during the) First Quarter Storm, I came home maybe 100 miles to the left of Marcos.

Well, if I had met President Marcos before I left for the US, I would have probably given him the benefit of the doubt. But after I came home, I probably would have told him where to go. Biased na talaga ako.

That is one sad development I keep hearing about [the youth today]. No consciousness about [Martial Law], how it was during those dark years.

When I arrived back [in Manila] on December 30 (or January), I signed up with Ayala

Corporation. But on my way down [to their offices], I hitched a ride with a fellow Bedan who was going to the BIR. When we got to the Supreme Court, I saw a rally being led by Roger Ayala, a good friend from the Ateneo. So I said, "I'm getting off. I want to join my kind of people." So even before I started with Ayala Corporation that very same day, I sent a letter of resignation.

If I had stayed with Ayala, maybe I would be in some plutocratic enclave now.

I founded the San Beda Free Legal Aid Clinic when I was in law school as a human rights lawyer, totally unknown in the legal zoo when I was a student. That probably was one reason why I won as Senator in 1987 without having to spend a single centavo of my own. The Filipino could be grateful. There's a saying in Spanish, "Amor con amor se paga (love is repaid with love)."

I'd rather earn psychic income because that was what drove me to law school in the first place—to make a difference for the poor, the obscure, and the oppressed. Of course, psychic income is not treated as legal tender in Cash & Carry, but it satisfies you in a more meaningful sense.

For one to take part in an electoral process in a dictatorship is to help forge the links in your own chains.

That is one sad development I keep hearing about [the youth today]. No consciousness about [Martial Law], how it was during those dark years. It was really terrifying, the first few years. If you have people like me (Ninoy Aquino and Ka Pepe Diokno) being detained for years, without any charges! Ka Pepe was released in 1974 and founded a free legal aid assistance group, which I also joined. Ninoy Aquino had a heart problem, and for the First Couple to release him, it was because they did not want to take any responsibility should anything happen to him here in the country. During the first elections [in] 1978, Ninoy Aquino lost to non-entities, and that was why we started a boycott movement, agreeing with the Greeks in 1974.

For one to take part in an electoral process in a dictatorship is to help forge the links in your own chains.

My family could not complain because I neglected all of them equally. I remember that my darling [wife] Dulce was so supportive and never questioned except for one Christmas. I attended a Christmas party for lawyers, a mere walking distance from home. So after dinner here, I disappeared and went to the party. When I came home, she did not berate me, but tears were falling softly from her eyes and she said, "Pati ba naman [sa] Pasko, wala kang panahon sa amin?" I had so many shortcomings as a husband and father because it was a time when I thought that the country should come first. Maybe it was poor judgment [on my part]. When she [died], I realized I was not the husband I should have been, even the father I should have been.

It wasn't hard to give up power, because I told my staff and myself, "We're here only for a short visit."

It wasn't hard to give up power, because I told my staff and myself, "We're here only for a short visit."

Someone once got my counsel and told me, "'Now I realize what a Jesuit priest taught us at the Ateneo: 'When you laugh, the whole world laughs with you. But [when] you weep, [you weep] alone.'"

All my life, imagine—topnotcher, cum laude, Harvard Law, full scholar—but I was not able to provide my family a home.

Now, finally I admit to being scared of one thing—long, lingering, hopeless illness. And if that happens to me, the little that we have would be spent on my care for nothing. So I just hope that the good Lord will continue to take care of me as another lily of the field. That has been the story of my life. I took seriously what I read in the Bible that the odds are worse for a rich man than a camel passing through the eye of a needle. So I just hope that next time I am admitted to Makati Med, that I would be treated gently. We were more than brothers. I feel only melancholy seeing my comrades pass away. Talagang lintik ang integrity ng mga iyan and wala pa kami compared to those we followed. How to bring back the glory days of the Senate is a big problem.

oooooo

24

JOKER, THE TEACHER, REMEMBERED

Oct 4, 2017

Yesterday was Joker P. Arroyo's second death anniversary. How he is sorely missed by some of us in our tiny human rights community, to which quarrelsome divisive cantankerous Prez Digong gives no importance, judging by his Kill-Pa-More Population Reduction Program. A healing unifier, he seems not.

From Joker we learned many things, like not standing on ceremony. He did not even want an hour or two in the Senate to observe a hallowed necrological tradition. He was a teacher in a real sense; he taught, by example, on how to stand on principle. Pleasant memories of military commissions and Supreme Court (SC) orals galore. Watching him was like peering over Juan Luna's shoulders while the latter was painting.

Yesterday was also World and Philippine Teachers' Day. Henry Brooks Adams said a teacher affects eternity. How true, in my case, from my teachers in Makati Elem in 1946-51 (accelerated, so I am a K-9 product, blest with excellent teachers). "Grammar is a matter of hearing," Mrs. Flora Cenidoza would stress.

Refined, in Rizal High, where Mrs. Maria Pineda taught us discipline. In San Beda, one is told to be like a music lover, jarred by a sour note hearing some grammatical infelicity, and so on and so forth. When I applied for admission in 1967 into Harvard Law, in my rinky-dink manual typewriter, I gave it fair warning to welcome me into the sacred precincts of Harvard Yard or someday it would be, haha, sorry. The yabang I got from the kanto but then Reggie Jackson said, "it ain't braggin' if you can back it up." Joe McMicking bragged on how he gentrified Makati when we met in 1968, in San Francisco, in the law firm I summer-clerked in. One lore is when asked how he raised the $10M - remember, 1968 values - needed for a project in Spain, he sniffed: "when you have it, you don't raise it."

But, I remember best his gracious parting shot, following an awkward start, in that if at any time I needed help, he was just a phone call away; I am glad that the Ayalas just honored him with a McMicking Courtyard. Shall we rename Makati Avenue as McMicking Avenue next? To me, he was another Teacher.

Maestros/as, maraming salamat po.

How sad that in 1978, after the Laban Metro Manila elections, pupils would have to say, "good morning, cheater," instead of "good morning, teacher." By marathon cheating starting in the 60's, the Marcoses ruined our values, processes and institutions. Digong now clears them without due process, without bothering to read what Swiss authorities say - as Raissa Robles has clearly written about more than once - of the unrepentant thieving family.

Imee was the usual charmer when we met recently in Swiss Inn; she was with the Ilocos Six, being, from where I sit, unfairly harassed by

Tsikboy Rudy Fariñas, a Corona impeachment megastar. Imee was the one asked by Archimedes Trajano in Mapua in 1977, in a manner which she didn't find amusing; he was escorted out by her sikyus. Hours later, he was found very very dead. All King Henry VI did was to ask "who would rid me of this boisterous/meddleso me priest?" ; four knights considered themselves told and sent Archbishop Thomas Becket to the Promised Land.

Imee and I met in Swiss (of all places) Inn last September 23 (of all dates). Digong should ask the Swiss authorities, particularly the Swiss Federal Court, or just ask super-journalist Raissa. And what about the tax liabilities of the Marcoses? They and Manny Pacquiao, along with Digong's Immigration brods, and the narco-police- generals, denounced on national radio-TV, appear to be selectively sheltered and harbored.

Back to World Teachers Day yesterday. Last Saturday I was pleasantly surprised by my brown-nosing sipsip haha Alabang law studes; at the end of class, just before eight pm, they sprang a cake. Then one of them (Tim Peralta) serenaded and played La Vie en Rose (Edith Piaf), on a violin, followed by As Time Goes By (from Casablanca). I requested Don't Cry for Me Argentina, which I was to hear later again that night in Solaire, along with La Vie en Rose, courtesy of Hiway 54 and 88.8, two very good bands.

As Tarrasch said, music, like love, like chess, has the power to make people happy.

Well, it was Saturday night: a client-couple, who happened to be there in Eclipse, the dance hall, picked up our tab. Merci. Earlier I got the good news that my eldest apo, Rene III*, 9, was home from Makati Med. Tres, Treasure when on his best behavior, and Stress, otherwise. Some days are perfect, but not too many. Last Saturday was one, for me.

One reason the rest couldn't be is Digong's traffic inutility. Another is he continues to talk too much. He has no Cabinet? Now he says no presidential run for Mayor Sara in 2022. Not serious, he says.

But, h**ow could we tell?

And Digong now says he will create a commission to probe the Ombudsman. Huh? On December 7, 2010, PNoy's EO No. 1 creating the Philippine Truth Commission to probe GMA was ruled unconstitutional, by her SC appointees (ten). We cannot single out anyone. And maybe rightly so. So, who then will police the police?

In 1967, I wrote an article in the San Beda Law Journal: "Yes, Virginia, There are Good Government Officials, But (A Filipino Ombudsman)." I there asked: "`Who will police the police?' the ominous question supposedly ventilated thousands of years ago by Cicero. . . . Looking at the same problem, Professor GS starts a piece with: `Quis custodiet ipsos custodes?' asked Juvenal which can be translated for our purposes as - who governs the government&# 39;?"

Digong now dares Chief Justice Meilou Sereno and Ombudsman Chit Carpio-Morales to resign with him. But, once the duo do, but not resigning himself, would he say "just joking?" - then name their replacements and keep his seat for fear of being charged with abandonment under Art. 238 of the Revised Penal Code, as the resignation has not been accepted. Who accepts the resignations of such high constitutional officials anyway? Our 1987-92 Congress did not act on my Senate Bill No. 1296 on resignations procedures. In the U.S., Prez Nixon submitted his resignation to the Secretary of State as provided by American law (3 U.S. Code Sec. 20). I find no such law here. We need one amid the most quarrelsome presidency we have been cursed with, in our Circular Firing Squad society. Our wounds are mostly self-inflicted.

Scarred, I for one do not want Rant-Rant-Rant Digong to resign, which may create more problems than it may solve. I want him to succeed, for everyone' s sake. But, he has to change. He should not be too talkative, onion-skinned, pugnacious and quarrelsome, like some fishwife (sexist today?) picking fights regularly; let the Cabinet work for their pay and perks. It seems any day he does not pick a fight with someone, he gets sick.

Sereno, Morales, Trillanes, Integrated Bar of the Philippines, Yellows (I am one, and proud to be so), Reds, Polka Dots, et al..

He should not cuss, not in public anyway, please, for the sake of the young; we try to rear them to be proper. We are a polite considerate sensitive people**; promdis, more so.

He has to stop EJKs, his perceived population reduction program. PNP Chief Bato de la Rosa boasts his police organization is admired by the world. Huh? What country has adopted our scorched-earth policy which has not succeeded anywhere? Imitation is the best form of flattery. If he's a hero in China, he should consider moving there as we only make him cry here. Critic Mon Tulfo and the bereaved Castillos do not seem to realize how lucky we are to have Bato.

I am not comfortable about Digong threatening people, like Deputy Ombudsman Melchor Arthur Carandang. If the guy were struck by lightning, Digong might court blame. "If the Philippines goes into chaos, I will come for you first," apostrophizing Carandang. Grave threats? Childish.

Who's causing the chaos by his needless confrontational behavior? Carandang must have peed in his pants and not surprisingly recanted, blaming the media. Remember what happened to Archbishop Thomas Becket.

Ang mapikon, talo, is an ironclad Kanto Boy Code. I was Lapiang Balat-Sibuyas Prez in the Senate. I know the feeling when one's honor is put on the line. But, Prezs should develop a thick hide, or go home. Digong can ape a tactful spokesman of his other Cabinet members seem invisible. He who is easily piqued, rants and cusses, has a weak case.

I never dissembled on my unexlained poverty. Unlike Digong I was not able to provide the family a home. All we seven siblings inherited was 161 square meters in Pasig which an aunt had given to my Daddy, and which we in turn gave to our two youngest siblings.

But, we had good teachers.

Had I been asked, I would have told my banks to make a full disclosure. I would not have threatened the Carandangs of our time.

Like I said, I expect transparent public servant Prez Digong to say, "I waive my bank and AMLC secrecy rights. What else can I do you?" Instead, tantrums.

Very occasionally some people ask me to run for Prez. And I'd say "di na nga makalakad, tatakbo pa?" - to drown out the question I hear from the back of the room "and of what country naman po kaya?"

Digong was given a gift and a burden. Use the gift and we share the pain and burden. Do not divide us. United, we are stronger.

Yesterday morning, my son, Atty. Rebo forwarded to me a text from Deng Bautista, a stalwart on our Vizconde Massacre defense panel, announcing "that Papa has answered the call of his heavenly Father to come home." Condolences. American Indians call it "homegoing."

While in Makati Elementary, I read Red Smith writing in this paper about the paths of glory leading but to the grave. Shall we quarrel less?

We will all go home someday.

Saguisag & Associates Lawyers 4045 Bigasan Street, Palanan 1235 Makati

oooooo

25

MANIFESTATIONS OF CREEPING DECAY

Sep 27, 2017

On frats, the right to associate, I believe, is in Sec. 8 of the Bill of Rights, Art. III - we, old fogies and relics and young blood, have formed Artikulo Tres, which was at the Luneta last September 21, the day of protest the Prez shrewdly hijacked - of the Constitution, which speaks of - "[t]he right of the people . . . to form associations, or societies for purposes not contrary to law."

Justice Secretary Vit Aguirre remarkably cites Sec. 4 on "the right of the people to assemble and petition the government for redress of grievances." Huh? But, a neophyte' s dream is mundane: camaraderie and passing the bar, not to air grievances. They assemble in secrecy.

As in a police stationhouse, the legislature must tell a guest, you have a right to remain silent. . . ." The Bill of Rights must not be checked at its gate. The right not to speak should not be ignored in Congress.

Anyway, recall the expensive full-page ads of Digong's frat (Lex Talionis, which the Prez calls "the law of the jungle" , but retaliation means an eye for an eye, parity or equivalence, also, where before it was 7, even 77, eyes, to one), flaunting how prosperous its members are. But, rich and poor all await our inevitable hour.

For Olympian Bedan cage star Bonnie Carbonnel it has come, per our sports scribe, my pal, our sports columnist Jude Roque, last Monday. Bonnie will be missed by those of us treated to the distinct flavor he added, particularly during the storied San Beda-Ateneo NCAA feud in the 60's, in full throttle by the time I entered the finest law school along the entire length and breadth of Mendiola. In recent years, I'd see him in San Beda games, assisting the coach in games redolent of excitement and gunpowder; and recall his monster performances, floating, pirouetting and jack-knifing.

I also recall Bedan Olympian Eddie Lim, standing at the corner of J.P. Laurel and Concepcion Aguila on January Sundays when we marked with our traditional procession the feast of Sto. Niño. And then he was also gone. Olympian Caloy Loyzaga followed later. Caloy was once elected Councilor in Manila at a time of more decorum.

In one training session of San Beda one night in storied Rizal Memorial, Coach Luli Rius raised his foot while I was interviewing him. Mrs. Rius was quick to say, "baje el pie!" And the feared Prussian Drillmaster considered himself told and literally put his foot down in sweet surrender: Josme! Takusa din po pala like me.

A genteel time it was. La cortesia no quita la valentia, courtesy does not detract from valor, Justice Eduardo Caguioa taught us.

It now disappoints to see on TV that while a formal hearing is going on, people are eating.

Proper? Why not just have a short lunch break of half an hour, max? But, breaks can reduce our solons' TV preening time, so I understand.

Now the Senate reportedly holds hearings at six pm, like last Monday, as Sherlock Holmeses. Would it not conflict with the usual business (lawmaking) time, which is not televised?

And no televised merienda sana during actual hearings; eating in the course of a congressional hearing detracts from the dignity and solemnity of the process. The famished could step out of camera range. In my time, no merienda even, after Kuya Teroy Laurel raised the issue if free food would be an unconstitutional addition under Sec. 10 of Art. VI of the Constitution to our pay (my take-home: P14,612.50. I had to bring my own baon. today, in Customs, revived is the tale that a new employee, on his first pay day, would blurt: "Ibig po nyong sabihin, may sweldo pa?" Tara-ra-ra-ran.)

When I visited Indonesia at the start of this millennium, I was told that cell phones were not allowed in the legislative session hall. I don't know if that is still the practice today.

It used to be said that 1) in Singapore, you deal across the table, 3) in the Philippines, under the table. and 3) in Indonesia, you include the table! Now Nos. 2 and 3 have been reversed? What is Digong's anti-corruption program other than prosecute ang mga di po ka-rancho?

What is his program to improve working conditions, on better pay with health care and pensions?

In Singapore, the leader is now a son of Lee Kwan Yew. Hmmmm. Maybe in 2022, it would be daughter Sara, with Alan Peter Cayetano(?), which just might be better than Manny Pacquiao-Mocha Uson? Or Sara-Mocha the way Digong is favoring the two. Susmariano!

In our free country, I like the way the Prez allows marches and assemblies, which disrupt skeds and disturb people, but, precisely, inconveniencing them is the whole point; we'd rather have them think of what they would rather not think about. The next generation, not only the next appointment. In our poor country, his war against drugs so far has been a war against the poor.

One point he and I are on the same page is the return of the Bells of Balangiga. Had I been in the Batasan for the last SONA, I would have stood up with Samar Cong. Raul Daza to cheer when Prez Digong mentioned the Bells, emphatically, in that they belong here. A forebear of Raul, Eugenio, was one of the wily patriotic leaders of the September 28, 1901 attack on the breakfasting U.S. soldiers which led to the move of two bells to Fort Warren just outside of Cheyenne.

There I saw them in 1992 (one is with an army unit in South Korea). In Cheyenne, was a family from UP, which the patriarch said stood for Useless People. When I'd mention this in the presence of my wife, a UP alum, I'd see to it I was not within ear-pinching distance.

Now, Digong says narco-politicians have been wiretapped. He has not said if judicial permission has been obtained. Now, the Palace says the Cabinet may choose what to disclose in SALN. Huh? More and more signs are emerging that not only does the Prez spit on the anti-dynasty clause in the Constitution. Like his idol, Macoy, he's behaving like a super-legislature and a one-man continuing constitutional convention.

Yawa! But, he can apply it to traffic. Last Tuesday, ANC's Lynda Jumilla had her program start at eight pm, on Balangiga, not the usual half an hour earlier. I came from another planet, Makati. Two hours and a half. My driver was so exhausted he could not report for work the next day.

If graded on traffic alone, Digong is a dismal failure, as Metro Manilans know, only too well.

My disbarment has been unsuccessfully sought more than once but it has never been publicized. Sec. 10 of Rule 139 of the Rules of Court says: "Confidential - Proceedings against attorneys shall be private and confidential except that the final order of the court shall be made public as in other cases coming before the court." So, why the publicity in the disbarment cases of Andy Bautista and Nilo Divina? What will the Supreme Court do to stop the confidentiality rule from being so brazenly disrespected?

Now I have been invited to a hearing in a Batasan Hall named after a living former speaker. This I warned about after a UP facility was illegally named after a living Macoy disciple, given R.A. No. 1059, forbidding naming public structures after the living.

Now the Palace has a new view on SALNs which it calls "redacted." From where I sit, "fake SALNs."

The Commission on Civil Service should also implement Sec. 7 of R.A. No. 3019, requiring the public servant to report "the amounts and sources of his income, the amounts of his personal and family expenses income earned, and the amount of income taxes paid for the next preceding fiscal year." If the noncompliance is widespread, as I suspect, beginning with the Prez, then let's have an amnesty with a warning that thereafter, violations would be strictly dealt with.

Shall we arrest the decay, now creeping, but may soon gallop?*

oooooo

26
September 11 and 21 follies and fallacies
September 22, 2017

I DON'T know why we mark September 21, 1972 as the day when Marcos inflicted martial law via Proclamation 1081. It was a normal enough Thursday. But, for numerologist Macoy, the number 7 and any of its multiples, like 21, were sacred. I don't know why we have to live with that gross historical falsification.

Worse is the Marcoses marking last September 11 as the kleptocratic dictator's alleged centennial. It was his 101st birth anniversary. My law studes have produced a copy of his birth certificate showing that he was born in Sarrat, Ilocos Norte in 1916, obtained by one Melvin dela Costa in 1998, issued by Local Civil Registrar Joan A. Duque. It would appear that ABS-CBN has published that historical fact. Normal, it seems, for the Marcoses to falsify.

Right after we ousted Marcos, Joe Mari Velez and Bob Swift filed the historic class suit against him in Hawaii, for an amalgam of reasons, such as exposing and denying a haven to gross human rights violators, to start the healing, etc. I was a Johnny come lately. Looking at the case file, I saw in the record, the testimony of Marcos, where he started by saying that he was born in 1916. Lying under oath is dealt with seriously in the US. Here, casual, no prosecution.

I asked my studes to validate that his centennial was last, not this, year. Last Sunday, it came from my resourceful San Beda Law Alabang studes. His centennial should have been last year. It may not be his fault but the anniversary rites last September 11 in the LNMB (Libingan Ng Mga Mandarambong at Berdugo?) was fake news. Somehow, I was reminded of that epitaph in Ireland: Here A Lawyer Lies Still. He probably misled his pliant family and loyalists to use 1917, 7 being a fave number of the numerologist. Or a multiple of it.

The resourceful studes I will give passing midterm marks. And anybody who can show that anyone in government filed last April proof that he has complied with Sec. 7 of RA 3019, by reporting 1) "amounts and sources of his income"; 2) "the amounts of his personal and family expenses"; and 3) "the amount of income taxes" paid the previous year, I will pass this semester. Permit me to doubt that the Prez et al. are in compliance in our scofflaw nation. He and Pulis Patola Bato de la Rosa even openly encourage duels, criminalized under Art. 261 of our Penal Code. Bato even urges arson, to burn where druggies live. "That's the way of a clown"?

The cruelest lies

Across the water, Sen. Manny Pacquiao has a chance to correct the damning judicial characterization that he was deceitful and unscrupulous in not seasonably disclosing his odds-changing shoulder injury. LA-based Fil-Am lawyer Ed Lopez said "the Los Angeles US District Court's decision dismissing the case, has been appealed to the US Federal 9th Circuit. Who knows, the 9th Circuit may think otherwise." It may reverse, or sustain and clear Manny fully. Else, on his failure to disclose his injury, Robert Louis Stevenson wrote that the cruelest lies are often told in silence. Shirazi Saadi said to be silent when it is time to speak is an irrevocable mistake (as well as to speak when it is time to be silent).

But, Digong, the lawyer, is correct in saying that son Pulong, vice mayor of Davao City (not mayor of vice), has the human and constitutional right not to speak in the Senate (and even not to exhibit his tattoo; hmmm, do Pulong and Sen. Sonny Trillanes have a common talkative kulasisi or lover?). The praxis in the US is to seek immunity from some court, which routinely cooperates with a co-equal branch. There, a resource person may invoke the Fifth Amendment (right to remain silent) but if immunity for him some court grants, he must talk.

Will Digong speak on the latest hazing death? His own Lex TalionisFraternitas often understandably speaks glowingly on the bonding paradise's perks. But, I wonder why he characterized Lex Talionis as the "law of the jungle." Did he have in mind our Red Lions – Kings of the NCAA jungle?

Lenny Villa was killed in frat hazing on February 11, 1991. His case was finally terminated in 2016, or 25(!) years later, courtesy of hardworking Chief Justice Meilou Sereno (ending the ordeal of the innocent accused, includingthat of our client, Zos Mendoza). It seems to me the Supreme Court's task or focus is "to decide cases," given the horrid delay in our courts, compounded by today's SC intramurals.

SALN non-compliance not heinous enough

SALNs are subject to a review and compliance procedure. The filer is given a chance to review and comply. The lead implementer or enforcer is the Civil Service Commission (Sec. 12), for administrative purposes, not the Office of the Ombudsman, which prosecutes, in case of recalcitrance if review and compliance would fail to correct or complete the SALN. That was my personal intent as Senate co-author and sponsor of RA 6713, which just might count for something, I would hope.

Given the light probationable penalties in RA 6713 (Sec. 11), it cannot be heinous enough to warrant the use of "the rusted blunderbuss" that is impeachment. Unfortunate CJ Rene Corona's case was distinguishable as he was a post-midnight appointee, named by GMA who was supposed to be a mere caretaker, for a smooth transition, not an undertaker, for her successor, then known (May 17, 2010, PNoy had won). That Senate Prez JPE was bribed by PNoy to convict is for the comic page. Seventeen other senators voted to convict with him.

Were I to take a psycho test, I'd probably flunk. I may be no raving maniac but I fought martial law from pre-Day One and even some kin and friends thought my headhad not been properly and tightly screwed on. Wifey Dulce was in support which was all that mattered. In January 1987, I was handed a signed Supreme Court appointment. I was 47. I turned it down, without even telling Bosswoman Dulce. For the little I had done, I always thought that serving the people was its own reward. To some, weird, even insane.

I doubt that anyone should be humiliated by pressing on the issue of one's sanity. To aspire to be an overworked, overcriticized, underpaid and under-appreciated public servant, and impeached at the end of the day, should not be the New Abnormal. The SC should decide cases, and not behave or be seen as a Circular Firing Squad.

The end of the beginning

September 21, 1972 was a Thursday. Ho-hum. September 22, Friday, was when JPE falsely claimed to have been ambushed; hours later, Pepe Diokno and NinoyAquino were arrested. September 23 was when the people felt the sting of martial law. No newspapers, no radio-TV, no long hair, curfew, and the long night began.

The Dioknos and Aquinos I joined at EDSA on September 23, 1972, and on February 22, 1986, JPE, FVR and Gringo crossed over from the wrong side of EDSA and joined the suffering people the military had long kicked around.

Ninoy, I met only once, in 1982, at Harvard in Cambridge and in his Newton home. We talked for about 10 hours, meaning he spoke for nine hours and 45 minutes. I spoke from time to time to remind him I was not part of the furniture, in my fascination with a consummate conversationalist. Talk of gift of gab. The first time he called me, in a Boston hotel, he made me feel like a long-lost fellow Bedan friend. "`Neeee!" The first time I saw him was when he was San Beda's fiery riveting 1964 commencement speaker. But, I remember better Amalia Fuentes going on stage with a graduating nephew, with her even more riveting eloquent body English.

Anyway, February 15, 1986 was not the end of ML. It was the end of the beginning (Churchill), of August 21, 1983, when Ninoy was salvaged at the airport, exactly as his mother had foreseen. As Danish-American pastor Kristian Ostergaard wrote —

That cause can neither be lost nor stayed
Which takes the course of what God has made;
And is not trusting in walls and towers,
But slowly growing from seeds to flowers...

Thereby itself like a tree it shows;
That high it reaches, as deep it grows;
And when the storms are its branches shaking,
It deeper root in the soil is taking.

Be then no more by a storm dismayed,
For by it the full-grown seeds are laid;
And though the tree by its might it shatters,
What then, if thousands of seeds it scatters?

There's a lesson for everyone, particularly the ruling class, here.

oooooo

27
Fighting Down his Weight
Sep 13, 2017

Prez Digong has a good Cabinet. He should make better use of it. He shouldn't have to fight down his weight. Thus, his needless monologues and quarrels with certain Senators who are better dealt with say, by Executive Secretary Bingbong Medialdea, Justice Secretary Vit Aguirre or Presidential Legal Counsel Sal Panelo.

He should give up some of the limelight so he can reflect more. He cannot for instance announce that an emissary of the Marcoses offered to return ill-gotten wealth and then dissemble, with little wiggle room. (It was like Bato de la Rosa saying no more jueteng after 15 days. Anti-poor governance by braggadocio. Casino rollers, high and low, untouched.

Fighting Sonny Trillanes can be handled by Digong ally Flash Gordon, trained and coached by Digong sidekick Manny Pacquiao who   thrives and shines in the Red-Light District of Sports (i.e., boxing, per Jimmy Cannon) or the Manly Art of Modified Murder (W.O. McGeehan). (He shrewdly
massages Hurricane Digong's ego, so no order to the taxman to ask questions about Clever Manny's supposed billions in tax arrears, per ex-BIR Chief Kim Henares.)

Indeed Super-Boxer Manny has won again, but why the local silence?

Last August 25, or three weeks ago, a U.S. District Court dismissed damage suits against Manny, Floyd Mayweather and their camps. Numerous plaintiffs had alleged being gypped or defrauded by the failure of both camps to inform the public of Manny's shoulder injury which should have been known also by Floyd's supposed mole in Manny's camp.

The District Court ruling last month on the May 2, 2015 bout concluded:

"The Court is sympathetic to the fact that many boxing fans felt DECEIVED by the statements and omissions made by the Fight's participants and promoters. The proper remedy for such UNSCRUPULOUS behavior when it implicates the core of athletic competition, however, is not a legal one. Disappointed fans may demand that fighters be more transparent in the future, lobby their state athletic commissions to impose more stringent pre-fight medical screenings and disclosure requirements, or even stop watching boxing altogether. They may not, however, sustain a class-action lawsuit. [CAPS ADDED.]

"In this case, Plaintiffs ultimately received what they paid for, namely: the right to view a boxing match, . . . sanctioned and regulated by the Nevada State Athletic Commission. Plaintiffs had no legally protected interest or right to see an exciting fight, a fight between two totally healthy and fully prepared boxers, or a fight that lived up to the significant pre-fight hype."

"Deceit" or "unscrupulous behavior" may be typical in boxing. Not for nothing is it called "the red light district of sports. "Sales talk" by snake oil salesmen is OK then?

But, I have to wonder why no local reporting I saw of a development of weeks ago as of late this week? I have a copy of the edifying ruling, courtesy of LA-based Fil-Am lawyer Ed Lopez, which ruling may or may not be appealed by any of the various plaintiffs.

I wish media would also verify whether last Monday was really the centennial or 101st birth anniversary of Marcos. 1916 was the year indicated by Marcos in the human rights class suit in Hawaii in 1986, if my memory is true. My efforts, and my studes', to secure a certified true copy of his birth certificate in the National Statistics Office and from the Ilocos have not worked.

This being Macoy's birth week, I also wish no American official would again say we are a country of millions of cowards and one SOB. And as I would add, in the 80's, "and one B." The Marcoses ruined our values, institutions and processes. This lesson we must remember. Jorge Santayana warned that those who do not remember the past are condemned to repeat it.

Imee says the Marcoses are in their winter. Politically, may they stay there forever. May they shine in philanthropy, say by helping fund our free education program under a law which was enacted in violation of the common-sense constitutional requirement of a treasury certification of availability of funds or a corresponding fund-raising scheme. From where

I sit, the law so irresponsibly passed is unconstitutional and free education is not quality education. "I have signed the law, go find the funding," boomed Digong. Cheap shot.

A popular chant we had in the dark years was MARCOS! HITLER! DIKTADOR! TUTA! or some such.

Today we have a Prez who insensitively sandbags his guests to do the clenched fist gesture with him, aping Hitler and his troopers, to the embarrassment of an Aussie official who got hammered for his thoughtless imitation. Only Pinoys he should ask to join him do the fascistic stance. We are certified cowards. And the Prez sees human rights addicts as a lower form of animal life, instead of co-workers for justice. Yet, he remains popular and populist. How many more guests will he embarrass?

But, my mantra is I do wish him to succeed as his success is yours and mine, everyone's. But ML? Again? Never Never Never Again!

And, hope springs eternal. If this be winter now, for human rights - P1,000.00 for the Commission on Human Rights - the poet asks the wild west wind, surely spring cannot be far behind? Digong will right the wrong, through his Senate Echoes, and get the credit.

The impeachment and conviction of Chief Justice (CJ) Rene Corona - his bitter winter in life - continues to be discredited by allegations that the Senate was bribed. You mean Presiding Officer Juan Ponce Enrile was, and did Noynoy a favor? I admired the skill of JPE in thwarting the defense maneuvers. To me CJ Rene validated the hoary maxim that a lawyer who defends himself has a fool for a client; the defense also may have erred when it decided to present evidence. It could just have rested when the prosecution rested nd Rene could have been acquitted or lost by a vote closer than 18-3. 18 "bribees?"

But then Rene took the stand and shot himself in the foot. Then the defense called Ombudsman Chit Carpio-Morales who had done her homework. Again in violation of a basic examination principle, whether on direct or cross, taught in basic Trial Technique: do not ask a question the answer to which you don't already know. So Ombudsman Chit went to town on Rene's dollar deposits provided by the Anti-Money Laundering Council, required to be reported in the Salonga Law, R.A. No. 6713, which I co-authored and sponsored on the floor. The defense misspoke, rendered Rene jobless, and broke his spirit.

The current spectacle of the Supreme Court supplying proofs of intramurals is sad and shows how low it has fallen from pre-ML years. One Kenkoy charge has to do with the purchase of a bullet-proof vehicle for the Supreme Court to be used by the CJ. It seems to cheapen the process. That the members want to be heard on personnel appointments seems too petty for impeachment. Their job is simply "to decide cases," as a U.S. Supreme Court nominee, footballer Byron T. White, famously told the Senate in 1962 when asked how he envisioned the SC's role to be. To leak info and "evidence" is not part of its lofty function. Such repeated leakage to our resourceful and blameless Jomar

Canlas causes damage in lessening the candid cross-fertilization of ideas in devil's advocacy. Power-sharing slows down adjudication.

Imee now says the Marcoses are in their winter.(?) Politically, may they stay there forever, like Hitler. They have damaged us enough. Philanthropy is where they can rise and shine, scintillate even, say by funding, say, Digong's free education program, for which there is no money now, given the various valid competing claims on our scarce resources. Our politicians are so populist, looking at the next election, not the next generation.

But, again, hope springs eternal. If this be winter now, for education and human rights, springtime cannot be far behind.

ooooo

28
Kill-Pa-More Administration? The Tagubas
August 24, 2017

What should come out tom, another potpourri/medley

* Kian delos Santos was well, just 17, if you know what I mean, and the way he looked, was way beyond compare. Very very dead he was. *

* No, we are not reprising the Beatles.*

* It is not in the national interest, in my view, to pressure Prez Digong to quit, given his overwhelming mandate last year. He must succeed.
He must not fail. Else, we all lose. *

* It is however in the national interest to pressure him to abandon his failed, bloody, messy anti-poor drug policy which has not succeeded
anywhere. *

* The short and simple annals of the poor matter. *

* No matter Kian's background, his seeming rub-out looks indefensible. As was the case of Ka Lando Olalia and his driver, Leonor Alay-Ay, in 1986, apparently done in by RAM (Rebolusyonaryong Alyansang Makabansa) leaders we met in 1985, when we were much younger and fresher; it was not about money but a better nation we furtively broke bread for.*

* In our old age, RAM now reportedly seeks amnesty with back pay from Digong, with his well-known soft spot for the police and the military.
Fine, but what about Ka Lando and his driver, murdered so cruelly? Ka Lando's mouth was wide open when found, grimacing in pain.*

* RAM met with Digong and may get what it wants - amnesty and back pay - in a Kill-Pa-More administration. Another hedge against coups?*

* RAM never staged a single successful coup. In February 1986, the People rescued the trapped group from being barbecued in their

failed coup attempt. Cardinal Sin and Butz Aquino asked the people to support and rescue RAM, helpless, retreating, not attacking. Entire families were   at EDSA, asking what they could do for the country.*

* A bright shining moment. *

* Now, RAM asks what the country could do for them. *

* Just turned 78, I know how it is to be ageing and ailing. Hospitalization and medicine and professional charges are costly so I try to be understanding. But, what about Ka Lando and his driver? (Not to mention the civilians arrogant RAM killed just for showing support for duly-constituted authority?) *

* It was on November 13, 1986, when Kilusang Mayo Uno (KMU) leader Lando and his driver were found in Antipolo. Their bodies had been

mutilated beyond recognition. A scar on Ka Lando's leg was the only mark that confirmed his identity. *

* The NBI, in its report to Prez Cory in 1986, said the killings were a prelude to "God Save the Queen," a supposed coup plot by RAM to   rid   the Aquino Cabinet of left-leaning members. *

* In January 1998, the Department of Justice (DOJ) filed a case as a new witness, former T/Sgt. Medardo Dumlao Barreto came forward,   implicating several RAM leaders in the surveillance and abduction of the victims. Barreto said he surfaced out of fear as several military men who had known

about the murders were ordered killed or mysteriously died. Dead men tell no tales. (But, for Kian there is CCTV, today, as well as brave live
eyewitnesses.)*
	* In May 1998, a five-man DOJ panel filed two separate cases of murder against 13 RAM members in the Antipolo Regional Trial Court. Among						those
charged were retired Colonels Eduardo "Red" Kapunan and Oscar "Tirso" Legaspi, a fellow Bedan. (Another fellow Bedan, Labor Minister Bobbit
Sanchez, the original MABINI chair, had left the country on a tip, and survived, unlike Ka Lando.)
*

	* Red and Tirso sought immunity from prosecution, arguing that Proc. No. 347 granted by FVR to rebel soldiers "extinguished their criminal
liability." They said political assassinations, such as the Olalia-Alay-ay double murder case, could have been part of simulated events intended to create an unstable situation favorable for a coup. In 2009, the Supreme Court dismissed their petition and ordered the filing of murder charges.*
	* In February 2012, the Antipolo City Regional Trial Court issued arrest warrants against thirteen defendants. On July 24, Perez surrendered
and later pled "not guilty" to the murder charges. The two cases are now pending in Taytay. *
	* I have no objection to amnestying RAM, which did its invaluable part in ousting Macoy, but

a measure of justice is also owed Ka Lando, et al..*

* A cussing Kill-Pa-More President and a sadistic RAM aren't, and do not represent, what we are as a people.*

* Last August 21, there was another gathering of millennials (and "perennials," added one who looked like Reli German). Our hairline and

ranks are thinning and many have gone to a better place, with no shoddy and bloody police operations.*

* Last Tuesday, for instance, I heard from Philip Suzara of the April 6 Liberation Movement that, Ed Olaguer, of the Light-A-Fire Movement, aided by courageous heroes Al Yuchengco and Mon Diaz, is gone. Condolences. Philip is a first cousin of Jinky Suzara, who married Gary Lewis, a son of iconic Jerry Lewis, a fave in our youth, also gone. Jerry made us laugh while Digong makes us cry, in the human rights sector, and now, elsewhere *

* Digong should stop scaring human rights advocates - we aren't his enemies - even if long ago, we mastered the art of pretending not to be afraid.*

* That is one lesson he should have learned by now. We leave everything to the Lord and can pretend to be unafraid. *

* I am not now for ousting him but he must change and show some respect for the human rights to life and dignity.*

* Ninoy belonged to the elite, scared and angered by what happened on August 21, 1983. When we in the opposition met in the home of

Esto and Maur Lichauco on August 7, 1983, we all looked forward to August 21. All save a Rand expert who said Ninoy would be killed at the airport, instead of being taken back to a prison cell. Naaah, Macoy wasn't that stupid. I would openly concede then that he was a criminal genius. Back to Fort Bonifacio, we said. *

* We asked Tita or Dona Aurora what she thought and she said she agreed with the think tank expert, her son would be killed at the airport. Huh, why Tita? She said, "kutob ng ina." *

* Anyway, because of the salvaging, I got to meet courageous Mrs. Soledad Duterte, Digong's Mom, who was among those who led the Yellow Friday movement in Davao City, for Justice for Aquino Justice for All (JAJA). *

* Where is the elite today? Just another day in the office, absent the economic crisis of 1983-86? Where is Makati Business? The Integrated/Inutil(?) Bar of the Philippines? The Philconsa?*

* Meantime, the Senate in a bipartisan move quickly caucused on EJKs. The House? Silent. BTW, has some Senator asked if Mark Taguba, a San Beda Alabang grade school alum, is related to famed Fil-Am U.S. Maj. Gen. Antonio Taguba who reported on military abuse in the Al Ghraib prison? Whistle blowing is in the blood? I have asked my studes to trace the connection, if any, the surname not being common. (I had a law stude nicknamed Taguba, Class '66, who migrated to the U.S., where we met decades ago.)*

* Anyway, for-from-elitist Kian, yagit. has done us the favor of stopping Kill-Pa-More, for now at least. Seemingly. And of making Digong stop saying "I have your back." But, he has no business talking of the guilt or anyone, not of the cops', not of Sen. Leila's, given the powerful effect of presidential rhetoric on human conduct. Just say "follow the evidence and let the system work."*

* One Caloocan prosecutor fell all over himself making sipsip, lawyered for the cops, saying what he thought the unpredictable Digong had

wanted to hear. Nabuking. Belat.*

* When Prez Nixon condemned Charles Manson, et al., for the grisly slaying of Sharon Tate, et al., Tricky Dick got hammered all over. The

White House quickly apologized and said Nixon had not meant to prejudge anyone. See Vincent Bugliosi' s Helter Skelter.*

* Here the cops and Leila cannot expect a fair hearing. Mistrial, I fear, which could lead to dismissal, assuming fear and ambition would not get in the way. The load is heavy enough without a madaldal Prez interloping, encroaching and intruding.*

ooooo

29
Hitler's 'Sieg Heil';
Immunity
August 30, 2017,

Prez Digong making the clenched fist gesture with visiting Aussie spymaster Nick Warner was embarrassingly reminiscent of what Hitler's troopers would do. For our Prez to sandbag a guest to do Hitler's infamous "sieg heil" gesture with him is insensitive. Flak would follow. I agree that the gesture seems "entirely inappropriate" . The gesture is illegal in Germany. But dis is d Pilipins? *

It may bespeak our ignorance of its Hitlerian provenance or our gross insensitivity. It reminds us of the MARCOS! HITLER! DIKTADOR! TUTA chant of the Dark Years.

I don't know if the middle and upper classes really feel safer today. I doubt that the masses do, given the anti-poor thrust of failed drug campaigns. Can one imagine Tokhang and house-to-house drug testing in unique Forbes Park? Only in our countless Pobres Parks are these inflicted.

The death certificate of Kian may state as cause of death: Duterte' s Anti-Poor program, which at the least occasioned, if not caused, his demise. On whose hands is the blood?*

So much needless divisive anger and enmity in a non-healing presidency. Sabong in the Supreme Court. Sabong in the Comelec. A seeming catfight between PAO and a Senate member. Also PAO versus NBI. Also the Ombudsman? They are co-workers in government?

Non-lawyer presidential spokesperson Ernesto Abella says trust the system, a sea change from what lawyers Duterte, Aguirre, Calida   and Panelo do, condemning personalities critical of the Prez.

Digong met Kian's parents. Good. He is Prez of all the people.

But why make them do "sieg heil?" Then he sends Chief Inspector Jovie Espenido to Iloilo City whose Mayor is said to be in some narco-list. Why not simply prosecute him, if the State really has the evidence? Iloilo City Mayor Jed Patrick Mabilog is in no hurry to go to the Promised Land — or where his foes tell him to go. He is vocal, not silent, about wanting to see the Prez so he can sleep again. As it is he is seen or misperceived as a Dead Man Walking, with a death warrant. Jovie may yet be remembered as a new Jovito Palparan or Rolando Abadilla, seen as butcherss.

A suspect in a stationhouse is reminded that he has the right to remain silent, a human and constitutional right seemingly checked at the Senate door in the Kian investigation, among other probes. The Senate Committee on Public Order and Drugs is supposed to probe in aid of legislation. Yet, we have well-meaning Sen. Manny Pacquiao saying to a cop: "If you don't talk when the public here is watching, you'll really be seen as guilty." He should have shown some respect for the Bill of Rights. Senators are sworn to uphold it, a document of distrust in powerful governors, and should correct, not enhance, misperceptions.

Even a rookie cop Mirandizes a suspect in custody: "You have the right to remain silent, etc.," showing due regard for the Bill of Rights, so disrespected in the House and Senate, which should work out immunity before making a guest become the tool of his own damnation. Else, they are like Torquemadas of the Inquisition, doing the best thinking and practice of the middle ages.

Under U.S. federal law, which may guide us here, Congress may work for immunity to witnesses who testify at congressional hearings, following a certain procedure. If two-thirds of the members of a committee vote to grant it, a request goes to a federal judge, who must issue an order granting immunity. Once granted, nothing the witness says can be used in a criminal prosecution against him.

Congress itself cannot grant immunity in the U.S.

There, Congressional staff will typically talk with the Justice Department before deciding what to do. And before granting immunity,

Congress will insist on knowing what the witness would say, which is usually in the form of a written proffer. Staff will first coordinate with the prospective resource person, which common sense dictates, but is not done here. There is a rush to grandstand, preen and torment.

I trained in Arnold & Porter and know a bit about such routine prior coordination. I would attend Senate hearings in the U.S. Congress as a water boy of sorts assisting senior counsel, such as Joe Califano (he had three secretaries - including a Miss Connecticut – and he later became a Cabinet Member in the Carter administration**). The courtesy and dignity "all around won't ever be beyond easy recall".

Why the need for immunity? Because without it, a witness in the U.S. can refuse to answer questions citing the Fifth Amendment protection
against self-incrimination. Once immunity is granted, the witness must answer. But, the U.S. Congress rarely grants immunity. The last time was
2007, when a Justice Department aide was called to testify about the firings of U.S. attorneys, I am told by Fil-Am lawyer Chuck Medel.

Our wild probes, so directionless and insensitive, drove two guests to suicide.

We speak above of procedural due process. For substantive due process, Uber paid a humongous fine of P190M - for conveniencing the
public? On what legally tenable, intellectually respectable and psychologically satisfying basis? But, moot and academic as Uber has paid. No Uber-da-bakod multa po sana, ha? No payment under protest for a test case?

Anyway, Digong has no known or ballyhooed program to alleviate our traffic woes, now worse than ever. He just does not talk about it. No way out? We may have to agree that always telling the truth may not work or be advisable if we are to maintain relationships in the real world, says Nick Hornby in Fever Pitch. You don't tell a mother about the appearance of a baby with a face only she could love. Be kind.

On truth telling, Comelec chief Andy Bautista supposedly lied in his SALN. R.A. No. 3019 and R.A. No. 6713 coexist. There is a report that someone in Mindanao has been charged by the Ombudsman with violating both. I am not privy to the details but some years ago, the Commission on Civil Service, if memory serves, decided to change its format to add what Sec. 7 of the Tolentino Law requires of a public servant, to include ". . . a statement of the amount and sources of his income, the amounts and sources of his income, the amounts of his personal and family expenses and the amount of income taxes paid for the next preceding calendar year." A good clause. I doubt that Andy Bautista has complied. Indeed, is anyone among our 1,600,000 civil servants in compliance?

Year after year I challenge my stude to show me a form showing compliance by anyone. No one has been able to, despite the promise to pass on that feat alone. I bet Digong does not comply with said excerpt from Sec. 7 (but complies with Sec. 8 of the Salonga Law I sponsored and defended on the floor). I have a copy of his SALN. He names some seven kin in government but does not state who is an asset and who is a liability.

Before charging anyone for violating Sec. 8, the public servant concerned must be given a fair chance to correct and tell the truth. My/our intent was to punish recalcitrance. The law is more administrative than punitive. But, our law made jobless Chief Justice Rene Corona, a post-midnight appointee named on May 17, 2010. GMA was supposed to be just a caretaker then; a new Prez had been elected.

Indeed the ban on midnight appointments starts two months before the election. Antedating seems to happen however so that a new Constitution should say only appointments made and published before the interdicted period would be valid, to plug a loophole in the 1987 Constitution which speaks incidentally about ill-gotten wealth.

Digong said an emissary of the Marcoses offered to return their loot in the billions with some gold bars to boot. We are told however that for every five things he says, to take seriously only two, with three for the comic page. Criminal genius, I have often said of Macoy, which could spread in the family by osmosis or descent. I am incredulous, as I write.

Let us see if we have front page (40%) or comic page (60%) stuff here. Statesman? Or comedian? Anyway, we again chant, "nakaw na yaman, ibalik sa bayan."

The Marcoses may be the last ones to know, as it were, but trust Digong to make things happen.

"Ma'am, kahiyaan na po ito, labi ni Sir, I'm under pressure to return to Batac, sabi ni Mamagawin ko po."

The Art of the Sandbag.

And The Deal. Libingan.

ooooo

30
Where is the National Security Council
July 13, 2017

Will Prez Duterte rely on his generals on how long martial law (ML) in Mindanao would last? Does he not see wisdom in Clemenceau's cautionary

counsel that war is too important to leave to the generals? Civilian supremacy is our lodestar (but please, not civilians like Speaker Bebot Alvarez who even now says ML till 2022. Josme!)

This paper bannered yesterday that Digong may ask Communist Russia for help. Land-grabber Communist China has donated arms. I doubt if such would boost the morale of our troops who see these countries as giving aid and comfort to our local Commies who kill our soldiers.

On Marawi, so Digong now sees the beginning of the end? I see only a Churchillian end of the beginning.

Military Intelligence (MI) failed on the preparation and entry of the Mautes, hence, the wrong time for Digong to visit Russia. It failed in assessing how long the Battle of Marawi would last. Digong should be with the people, not only with the military. He ignores the Lanao del Sur Integrated Bar of the Philippines (IBP) chapter, and Congress, and vowed to ignore the Supreme Court, in case of an adverse ruling. Only the

military
he would heed. Civilian supremacy gone.

And just why do we not hear about the National Security Council (SC) being convened? Is the Palace allergic to contrary views? The Palace wants unanimity behind the Prez but the compulsory unification of opinion, no matter how subtle, can only lead to the unanimity of the graveyard, to filch from Justice Jackson. That is why we have an NSC, which the Prez has not convened, as it is not pliable or predictable, unlike Congress or the military.

NSC members may be Voices, not Echoes. Better for Digong to convene the NSC than rely on the wimpy Chuwari-Wari Choirs in the Bigger House and the supposedly Better House.

Right on, Sonny Trillanes, for preserving a semblance of independence of the Senate, helping save the institution.

Military Intelligence (MI) bombed in not knowing about the May 23, 2017 Maute terrorism start. So, Digong flew to Russia. MI kept predicting
the Marawi end in weeks and again only proved to be a contradiction in terms. We are now on our eighth week.

I believe the jury is still out on the Supreme Court (SC) 11-3-1 voting on ML. I would not agree now that Justice Leonen's dissent is "baseless, " or some such.

Too soon? We may need to await the wisdom of a new day. My own gut feel is that if Leonen is not our new Teehankee, he could be our   new consistent Concepcion or Zaldivar. Or the inconsistent Fernando.

Do we have, today, a Resplendent, or Craven, Eleven?

Also premature of course.

All Supreme Court Justices (SC) answer to history.

On March 31, 1973, six SC Justices (Makalintal, Castro, Barredo, Makasiar, Antonio and Esguerra) prevailed, in ruling that "there is no further judicial obstacle to the new Constitution being considered in force and effect." I don't believe history has been kind to the six in letting the Siopao Constitution enter into force (in the Barangay Citizens Assemblies of January 17, 1973, the attendees were asked "sino sa inyo ang may gusto ng siopao?" Hands raised were counted as "yes" votes.).

Chief Justice Concepcion, joined in dissent by Zaldivar, Fernando and Teehankee, reportedly stopped reporting for work after March 31, 1973.

I regret that not enough importance may have been given to the on-the-ground position of the courageous IBP Lanao del Sur Chapter, feet not planted firmly in midair, which denounced government abuse.

But, the NPA is a bigger fish to fry. Digong is not wrong to negotiate with it. The NPA has been with us for decades, the Muslims warriors, centuries. As JFK said, not to fear to negotiate but not to negotiate out of fear.

On negotiations, Tocayo Rene Espina's assertion in his Bulletin column last Sunday that

Cory Aquino had a secret deal with the Commies (who had fought Marcos from the very start of martial law), I found astonishing. I recall our open repeated cries "Release All Political Detainees" - Palayain ang Lahat na Bilangong Pulitikal!" - which was a unifying slogan among all freedom fighters opposing martial law (ML) at the time. May   I reassure Tocayo Senator Rene that we had no secret agreement; the release of all prisoners of conscience was one vocal battle-cry and commitment of ours.

Right after Edsa'86, Uncle Jovy Salonga and I had two meetings in Club Filipino with Manongs FVR and JPE, as members of the Committee   on   the Immediate Release of Detainees. (Uncle was Chair; Joker Arroyo was another member but as Executive Secretary he was too busy returning the   salutes   of generals we had used to fight.) FVR was taciturn. JPE was passionate in opposition saying he could not "explain to my boys why those they had captured at great sacrifice would be freed." Or words to this effect, reflective of the military' s antipathy towards Commies?

My response was we'd lose all credibility if we would start by reneging on our long-time open and loud commitment to free all the freedom fighters who had dared to resist from the start, and suffered in detention.

Rene's Nacionalistas were in bed with Macoy from 1972 and 1980, which latter year was when Sen. Tanny Tañada, Juan T. David and I visited gutsy Erik, Rene's son, in a military camp, one late night. 1980 we boycotted after the 1978 cheating. Erik, a fellow Bedan who was, as I understood it, student council head, was campaigning for boycott. Arrested, Erik & Co. we visited in the dead of night in either Crame or Aguinaldo.

The Liberal Party, led by Gerry Roxas and Uncle Jovy, had fought martial law from the beginning. Rene's Nacionalista Party was in bed with Macoy from 1972 to 1980, with hormones raging, before they broke up.

Today, Senator Espina must be as dumbfounded as I to read that the Commission on Audit had found the present Senate not using its toilet paper enough, as it were. Hmmmm. No wonder.

Anyway, Rene is from Cebu. "Island in the Pacific" is said to have done wonders for Cebu; can we be creative and adapt/plagiarize a bit and use "Islands in the Pacific?" Or Harry Belafonte' s "Islands in the Sun?" DOT: no charge.

Farther down south, Muslim rebels are all over Mindanao. NPAs, all over the country, compared to 80 Mautes reportedly remaining in Marawi.

No, negotiations with brother Filipinos cannot be apodictically ruled out. Maybe lawyers can help. Digong is a lawyer but he may need the likes of James Donovan (Tom Hanks), the civilian corporate lawyer who deftly negotiated the release of Gary Powers and Frederic Pryor in Steven
Spielberg' s Bridge of Spies. (Not Bridge of Sighs, which we seem to have in more than one part of

the country, due to disasters, natural and man-made.)
Hanks was honored this week by the U.S. National Archives Foundation partly for his compelling performance in Bridge of Spies, among other films.

The Kanos and Russkies keep talking. Trump and Putin just met and have varying war stories of how it had gone.

In Digong's second year, he should make certain course corrections. Beginning with his bastos vocabulary, which does nothing positive for our image and raising our children?. No need either to give in to some anthropophagic urge to eat human liver. Will such weird bent or taste improve tourism?

Has the military done anything in Marawi it could not have done without ML? Now Super-Sipsip Speaker Bebot Alvarez suggests ML till the end
of time, Digong's, i.e., 2022, unless he again apes idol Macoy and goes on and on. Susmariano!

Time to go north, not south.

On another front, I was at the NCAA opening last Sunday. Battle field was the MOA Arena. Bedan Jay Ignacio, a Bedan fanatic assured me
last week that 2017 would be a walk in the park. Was I in near-shock when in the fourth quarter San Sebastian was ahead, until a late blitz mowed
down the gallant Stags. I would have been catatonic otherwise. Intelligence on the opposition we must have gotten from some General?

At halftime, I got a copy of a souvenir program edited by our fellow Times columnist Jude Roque (sports section). I learned there that Coach
Boyet Fernandez and I share being alums of the University of Negros Occidental-Recoleto s, in Bacolod, where I had my freshman law, after my AB
in San Beda, where I returned for the course balance.

I don't remember my parents riding shotgun in our studies and choices of profession. They just let us be.

Anyway, our win last Sunday was kinda ugly but I - a sore winner - took it. I wore a Golden Warriors cap sent by a brod from San Fran. That was the first and last time I would wear it.

I had with me in the MOA arena a new book (2017), to read during breaks: a Dorothy Day bio, "The World Will be Saved by Beauty [Dostoyevski]
- An Intimate Portrait of My Grandmother, " by Kate Hennesy. Catholic convert Dorothy committed many sins and indiscretions but with heart in the
right place, for the poor, may in fact be canonized. "Entertaining Angels" is a movie about this founder of the Catholic Worker movement.

She converted at 30, after a bohemian background.

There's hope for everyone then, Digong not excluded.

Would that we may not keep going south in so many respects, beginning with traffic, far worse than a year ago, on which he has said and done nothing, from where I sit. Absolutely.

But, if Dostoyevski is right on Beauty, we are saved. Just look around. Start with my apos. Fruit does not fall far from the tree.

Saguisag & Associates Lawyers 4045 Bigasan Street, Palanan 1235 Makati Office Nos. (+632) 551-6350 /833-4140 Fax No. (+632) 831-2276

ooooo

31

True and False Prophets
July 6, 2017

The time will come for history to judge our current Supreme Court (SC), which includes our paper's Justice Jomar Canlas, who I commend for
enterprise. Tunay, di po, bulaang propeta. He has done it again. I am again shocked and awed. Our SC leaks like a sieve and has done nothing about it
that I can see.

You wanna know how the SC would rule? Subscribe to the best paper in town.

In the Marcos era, we filed lost cases for winning causes, as depositions for history, and to make the other side doubt its moral premises - to be judged at a later time, in the calm of our study. The
Marcos SC is not remembered fondly today, for

its blind spot when it came to martial law (ML) cases (e.g.,the Ratification Cases of March 31, 1973,   a day of infamy; it was excellent otherwise elsewhere). Last Tuesday's majority ruling may satisfy the high feelings of the moment, in certain sectors, but in the sober afterglow may come the realization of a sorry constitutional "overreach", or folly, to paraphrase Justice Frank Murphy.

Rottweilers Speaker Bebot Alvarez and Rep. Rudy Fariñas, Digong's attack dogs, had threatened the SC (and the Court of Appeals) with impeachment complaints, etc.. Digong himself said he would rely more on the military and ignore an unfavorable verdict; egregious shades of Macoy. The judiciary, beleaguered on more than one side, by being bullied, arguably succumbed. Survival or self-preservation, after all, is the first law of mankind.

Those who do not remember the past, warned Jorge Santayana, are condemned to repeat it.

Sen. Tito Guingona, my fellow freedom fighter and Senate contempo, marked another birth anniversary last July 4 (his 89th). His sage counsel I have not forgotten: "deny, deny, deny, until you die." What used to be denied is now flaunted, very much in the open. Prez Digong does not deny, but even exhibits, if you know what I mean. Change has come, and I just may have to eat my heart out here.

Maybe after a year of governing by braggaddocio, arguably, our amazingly popular Prez - like Manny Pacquiao - should now consider Teddy Roosevelt' s sage counsel - "speak softly and carry a big stick," if we have the latter.

And stop misusing the "human rights salute" of the oppressed (clenched fist).

China's creeping baseless spurious Irredentism is reducing our territory. We are perceived as lambs meekly settling for its cheap bribe of firearms. We are not winning elsewhere, or so it seems, from where I sit, choked in traffic, worse than ever. A disaster was the "Battle of Brisbane," exposing certain Manny Pacquiao backers as false prophets.

The July 3, 2017 Time cover carried the caption or title "Battle of Marawi." After a year of Digong, we're again in the limelight. But, I am going on 78, born 1939; one marathon ML regime is enough for one who has survived martial misrule by the Japanese and the Marcoses.

Now, we seem to have a Police State. And the narcotics trade is back in Bilibid, resurgent, admits Injustice Secretary Vit Aguirre, courtesy of "tainted" cops. Mga Pulis Na Patola (PNP). A colossal disaster then, Digong's failed costly bloody hardline policy on drugs, which in fact has not succeeded anywhere else.

Will Thailand for instancereprise its spectacular failure? Who has copied Digong after a year? Human life and dignity continue to be respected elsewhere.

Has Digong's ascent from local Mayor, to the presidency, been good or bad karma for the nation? Aside from Honeylet Avanceña and his reported

two kulasisis in Davao City, where his children

are Mayor and Vice Mayor (the Durants' "paradise of pedigree"), and his alleged kalaguyo in Cagayan de Oro, his fellow Davaoeños and frat brods, how many of us can truly say "I am better off today than a year ago?" The killer traffic alone, costing us billions, affects and limits me, and I, with health issues, dread going out. Unaffected, has he said or done anything about it? Am I the only one left expressing concern over the Duterte dynasts?

(My pal, Ting San Diego, head of MAD - Movement Against Dynasties - was murdered in 2015.)

The Prez has to slow down his hectic social life that can kill a horse. He is 72, with health issues.

Aboard the Skyway bound for Muntinlupa last Friday, to lend my moral/immoral support to Senator Leila de Lima's legal team, the gridlocked Makati-bound traffic was horrid. Nothing like it a year ago. I was late for her hearing but FLAG-MABINI stalwart Alex Padilla was there. Alex should be in the Senate, as his father, Ambo, was (a star athlete, like Bill Bradley of the Knicks; they worked as full-time Senators and did not minimize the position as a sideline or hobby. Great Pretenders they were not).

Leila's crime? Criticizing Digong's human rights policies. Supposed she had been quiet or even joined the chuwari-wari choir? See the police generals and his BI brods. May advance pardons na, as promised?

To be fair, Digong is entitled to his fair share of rookie errors or lapses. But, positive change must come, beginning with bettering and refining his limited vocabulary. Has his continued cussing given us a better life? His audiences may stop applauding. Kumita na po 'yan.

And even if his hardline supporters saw a spectacular rookie year, should we be concerned about a sophomore jinx? Beginning with the Debacle in Brisbane?

The Time piece above concluded with a militant telling kin about his plan: "I will die." Our brave soldiers, patriots, with all due respect, serve to earn a living, by and large. How do we fight juramentados with the incentive that as martyrs, 70/71/72 virgins wait for them in paradise, distant promises of beauty untouched by the world? KJ me would want to know (my usual foolish questions, from an unhinged mind): these virgins, how old are they? How do they look? Does it explain why they have remained virgins? Sexist and anti-Muslim, you say? K, sorry. No fatwa please.

Did we have to destroy Marawi in order to save it? The city of Ben Pre was supposed to have been destroyed in order to save it during the Vietnam War. Another memorable Time cover was its February 1968 issue showing national police chief Nguyen Ngoc Loan shooting a handcuffed   Viet Cong. It won a Pulitzer for Kiwi Peter Arnett, who quoted destroy-and- save, and might have helped turn the tide of public opinion.

On February 7-8, 20,000 Muslims, along with Christians and aliens were killed in Jolo by our military. The suppressed media had no account   on it. Today, the alert militant press may save lives and protect other human rights in Marawi, grossly violated per the Lanao del Sur Integrated Bar of the Philippines chapter.

Military Intelligence may again have proven to be a contradiction in terms which may explain why Digong was in Russia when the Marawi   tragedy began.

Martial law continues to enjoy the brown-nosing support of those with legal problems and cases, save Leila who would not be in jail today had she kept quiet, or even apple-polished, the winning formula of those Digong and Injustice Secretary Vit choose not to go after. Selective Justice, administered with an evil eye and an uneven hand. Sen. Sonny Trillanes, a saving grace, to be punished for being a Voice, not an Echo?

After one year, traffic worse than ever. Malas po, which affected Manny Pacquiao. If his Wassisname? foe simply stood at the end of twelve rounds, he would not have lost, from where I sit, given the boasts and false prophecies of Manny's camp.

Boxing manager Joe Jacobs became famous for two quotes Manny could use: "I shoulda stood in bed." And "I wuz robbed."

If loser Manny, top House Absentee contender, is thinking of a rematch, the nation and the Senate might continue to be robbed. He has   to retire now and focus on his 2022 run for the presidency. There's hope for one who landed as No. 7 Senator after a dismal record in the House as   a Non-Performing Liability. But, he has to work very hard as a Senator now (Manong Ernie Maceda and I had perfect attendance in 1987-92, country above self) and share his billions with the Marawi refugees, after settling his tax issues.

Manny once promised to give up boxing to be a full-time public servant. But, he now treats Senate work as a diversion, sideline or hobby. His colleagues tolerate, instead of discipline, him, unethically damaging the institution. He is not the only one who needs to be taken to the woodshed?

Our decay continues. In my Senate stint in 1987-92, I proposed that we all work as Senators full-time, giving up our professional practice and businesses. It was dead in the water, understandably, as we would have had to settle for a take-home pay of P14,612.50.

Today, with all the extras and allowances the Senators reportedly get, it may be time to resurrect my proposal.

The consentidores can start with Manny, who had better stop whining, and thinking of another fight. They had better stop tolerating the spoiled brat, to help restore the dignity of the Senate as an institution.

He should be told that as prudent it is to know when to arrive so also is knowing when to leave. He should exit with part of the appreciative grateful bloodthirsty crowd still applauding.

He should settle his tax issues involving billions with the BIR (Pambansang Balasubas?).

And he should not fly out, and back, with an honor guard even. So much wastage of official resources.

Listen to Wifey Jinkee and Mommy Dionesia. The time has come. As a Senator, be a man of respect. Look at my City, which has, for a Mayora,
Abby Binay, who, we can see after her rookie year, goes by the star of non sibi sed aliis, not for ourselves, but others.

Saguisag & Associates Lawyers 4045 Bigasan Street, Palanan 1235 Makati Office

ooooo

32

Vive la difference!
Feb. 3, 2017

CORINNE Calvet may not ring a bell for my young readers, if any. She was a French actress. Voluptuous. In 1951 to 1955, I, as a Pasig Rizal Hi stude, kept hearing about her from an older Francophile classmate. With raging hormones, he just kept raving about her. In 1963, as a law grad, I saw Irma la Douce. (In 1969, I married my Dulce la Douce, my Mrs. Universe.) Today, how delightful to hear "La Vie en Rose." My little voulez vous, etc. French connection I got from auditing, briefly, in 1967, a French class at San Beda handled by Mlle. Odile Bresolette (?), where I picked up a little French. Un peu.

Miss France, Iris Mittenaere, tres ravissante, won as Miss Universe last Monday. Our pert bet, Maxine, was in the Top Six. Tres bien.

To France we owe liberte egalite fraternite (today, we may have to add sororite). What one law teacher taught us at San Beda was that on debating whether to give women the right to vote, in the French Parliament (Chambre des Deputes), an advocate, in peroration, supposedly boomed: "That is why, mes amis, we have to give women the right to vote, for after all, between men and women, there is but a little difference!" Whereupon, the entire male assemblage rose to its feet, and declared with effervescence, with that kind of passion that whips the blood: "Vive la difference!" The French explain why they kiss a woman's hand, "mon ami, you've to start somewhere." (Merci, Secretary George Shultz.)

Miss Universe reminds me that much of the known universe reacted negatively to Prez Trump's ban on the entry of certain nationals. We could have just kept quiet but instead Prez Digong openly supported the bigot, not helpful and comforting to our countless TNTs. Digong made the proper gesture though of welcoming any interested alien refugee, impractical as it may be; he could have cited the way MLQ welcomed the vilified and persecuted Jews, Quirino, the White Russians, and Marcos, et al., the Viets, Cambodians and Laotians. We should not depart from our civilized human rights tradition on refugees, of providing way stations, and not highlight our support for bigot Trump's racist interdiction, to our countrymen's prejudice.

The Pope Digong cussed is quoted to have said, one may not reject refugees and call himself a Christian. Recall the pixes of kids crying on rejection at the borders, which can tear one's heart by the roots.

Nice that government has moved because a SoKor was brutally victimized, but with lives of the local poor, collaterized as damaged, merely put in the back burner. It falls all over itself scrambling to give justice to an alien. Pero Pinoy, pobre, sori. So, wawa naman. Little in life, nothing in law.

But, Prez Digong, who vowed to "do justice to every man," can better allocate his time.

He should leave it to Executive Secretary Bingbong Medialdea and Justice Secretary Vit Aguirre, if need be, to prejudge and condemn people lest a mistrial be declared by a courageous judiciary. If the Prez announces X as guilty, and orders his arrest (usurping a judicial function), he leaves himself no wiggle room which an alter ego provides, and sandbags those below. Prez Nixon prejudged Charles Manson & Co. for the grisly slaying of actress Sharon Tate & Co in 1969. Widely assailed, the White House quickly apologized; it stressed that it was not Nixon's intent to prejudge the case. Here, our Prez prejudges all the time, as Macoy did. And the bar is so quiet, in the main, like the German lawyers in Hitler's time.

When I was in the Senate (1987-1992), we viewed the local police and the Philippine

Constabulary (PC) as allowing themselves to be goons of incumbents in their fiefdoms. (Fifty-one Pinoy constables joined the Kanos in the 1906 Bud Dajo massacre. Pure Pinoy troopers burned Jolo and killed 20,000 natives on February 7 to 8, 1974.) We decided to dissolve the PC, and create a national police force, to take over in time the domestic insurgency problem. The military would take care of national defense, and protect us from alien invaders (but in the West Philippine Sea dispute, we seem to have prevented China from raping us by simply lying back to enjoy it, for economic gain. PI! High-class prostitution. Now Digong asks China to help patrol our southern waters; Trojan seahorse?). 9/11 was not even a figment in our imagination in 1987-1992. The hope was that mayors won't have their own thugs in their turf in the way of private armies and lost commands (today, vigilantes).

The Philippine National Police (PNP) has a Special Action Force, to match the toughest of the tough in the AFP. It is not fair, it seems to me, for the Prez to blame Noynoy for allegedly sending in boys to do a man's job. Elite SAF troopers are not boys. Not Pulis Patolas at all. Men they are.

If Mamasapano is reinvestigated, it should not be limited to the gallant 44, but also to the Muslim civvies killed or injured, beginning with Sara, 5. Why not Mamasapano 67? Not only the fabled and favored 44 whose loved ones may try to begin to understand that when any trooper goes to enemy lair, it may mean "goodnight". The 44 have been recognized and rewarded for bagging Marwan, with $6 million on his head (did the bounty matter?). But, not the collateral damage. Nada from Manila, for Sara, et al. No audience with the Prez for her parents, both wounded in Mamasapano. By whom, it should be established.

The widows and PNoy critics may have their "alternative facts." Whew! Before Trump, "version" or "spin" would have done. Mine is that Pinoy answers to his conscience, his God and history. JPE to help send Noynoy to jail for treason, a war crime? Did JPE and Macoy commit arson and murder in sending troops to burn Jolo on February 7 to 8, 1974 and killing 20,000, shielded by a heavily censored media (e.g., Daily Suppress, Manila Bullshitin, etc..)?

If Noynoy had not been charged by the Ombudsman, it seems to me the remedy is to go to the Supreme Court, not the press. Not to politicize and try and convict by publicity. The local superstition is that our President is immune, as if we have royalty. Mga dugong bughaw. Lese majeste. Backward USA does not share our superstition and Prez Turumpong Kangkarot is now facing more than 75 lawsuits, with one from a woman (Summer Zervos) who claimed to have been improperly touched by the cad.

Impeachment of the Ombudsman seems out of the question. Her error, if any, could have been corrected by the Supreme Court if a proper petition had been timely filed after Digong took his oath, given the local undemocratic non-egalitarian legend of immunity for Prezs.

No Prez can worry about any actual police or military operation; he cannot micromanage troopers on the round. He is saddled with too many other pressing simultaneous concerns and cannot confine himself to a war room, for some war game. He answers to his conscience and to history. No one becomes god as President; he remains a fallible mortal, like, say, any coach in basketball. Infallibility is expected only of a Pope, in a limited context at that. And Alexander Pope wrote, "To err is human, . . ."

I do not believe in immunity for anyone in government; however, no one there, of course, can be held legally liable for any misjudgment in good faith, in the performance of his official duty or color of it, lest no one serve there anymore, if infallibility is required. The judge who erroneously convicted Hubert Webb & Co and made them stew in jail for more than 15 years, may not be sued, without more.

Secretary Vit Aguirre and I were together in the defense. I had to leave when the judge ordered four trial days a week (our small firm could not manage it) but the superb team of Vit, Mario Ongkiko and Demy Custodio, among others, simply appealed the conviction, and truth and justice prevailed, without going after her.

If this administration believes in presidential immunity, why has it not elevated the Ombudsman's ruling clearing Noynoy beginning June 30, 2016, when he stepped down? If no one had done it, ala eh, may natulog na naman po yata sa pansitan? The new administration, instead of bellyaching on supposed past failures and neglect, may be better off saying it would build on what it has inherited from Cory, FVR, Erap, GMA and PNoy, correct lapses, and lay down its share of bricks in the national cathedral being built.

It can for instance add to the highways that have made it easier for me to go to Baguio, La Union, Laguna and Batangas. I am told the way to my maternal hometown, Mauban, Quezon, is now concrete, all the way (192 kilometers). Smooth. And we take the smooth with the rough.

Arrogance of power of rulers we have no use for though. The new governors can exercise their bragging rights without demeaning their predecessors, particularly those who did not steal. And private initiative has been helpful. When I met Joe McMicking (JM) in the summer of 1968, in the San Francisco law firm I was summer-clerking in, he told me: "Young man, Makati as it is today, I built." Hambog, I thought. But, one may contrast Makati and Pasay (no JM). I will never forget his parting shot though (after insulting me at the start: "I don't like your weak voice. [Ouch] Be like me, when I whisper, my voice carries across the room." Yabang, I thought, and raised my voice, with some heat. "Better," he said, and after some time, he concluded: "If you ever need my help anytime anywhere in the future, I am just a phone call away." Right here. (He then sent fellow Bedan Mario Camacho to recruit me, another story.)

Generous SM, as well as the Ayalas, can rest content that it has done what JM did. Vision matters, punctuated by low-key humility.

Taguig was swampy when I had classmates from there in Rizal High (1951-1955; Nielsen Airport in Makati we'd get horse poo-poo for fertilizer when I was in Makati Elem, 1946-

1951, accelerated). Private initiative made the Global City what it is today on the basis of laws we passed in our time in Congress. This administration may be most hambog but then it ain't braggin' when you can back it up [Reggie Jackson), so, we wish it well. (It certainly is the most bloodstained; sana di na kill pa more.) Let us see whether it can give our many who are poor a better life, extracting a fraction of what the few who are rich have,

Oh Sadly, the cops are headed by Bato de la Rosa, who tells the world, embarrassingly, that harakiri is Korean. (Malaya Business Insight, Jan. 20, 2017, p. B3, col. 6.) He cannot even tell Korea from Japan and may not be aware of the reported continuing animus between the two great cultures, given Japan's barbarities. Bato has to study kamikaze and seppuku and the legend of the noble samurai before making another mistake. We can tell: his lips move. Same with his idol who believes he can order the arrest of anyone. Only courts can issue warrants, which Pulis Patolas may find an inconvenience. It took Bato but a semester to make the PNP a most feared and discredited entity, disrespected by the people.

Where has the rule of law gone? In the US, "immune" Trump is facing 75 lawsuits, one filed by gutsy celebrity lawyer Gloria Allred on behalf of Summer Zervous, for unwanted sexual touching. "But wanted here," our Prez may demur, coached by a fellow Killer, as in Lady Killer, Mon Tulfo.

We are different? If so, no "vive la difference!"

Some people around the Prez may not agree with EJKs and the return of the death penalty. If so, they should speak up, even in executive session or confidential memos, and not surrender their conscience to the state, to one who fancies himself as a 2017 Louis XIV, with his "l'Etat, c'est moi." "I am the State."

Trump just fired Acting Attorney General Sally Yates, reviving memories of defiant Antigone of ancient times and of the Saturday Night Massacre of Nixon when he let go AG Elliot Richardson and others in 1973. Those who left government landed on the right side of history.

The new elite should have realized by now that they seem to be validating, that "for every complex problem, there is a solution that is simple, neat and wrong." (TY, Timie Lim and Malou Tiquia, for "Uncertain Justice – The Roberts Court and the Constitution," by Laurence Tribe and Joshua Matz.)

oooooo

33
Lonely at the top; on moral stamina

Feb 22, 2017

A friend who attended last weekend's PMA rites where Digong spoke, found it weird that he would talk on a solemn occasion about his two wives (violative of the laws of God and man here) and his nostalgia for the quiet life of a Mayor.

As a fellow septuagenarian (I am 77, he, 71), I discern a sense of loneliness, particularly at the top. And since the cold spell began, I have been under the weather. I have had dizzy spells since last week. One of them came last Saturday, when I had to get up early to catch the tail end of the Luneta Walk for Life activity. I got there at past six for the 4-7 am affair but could not even get off my vehicle. Dizzy. I had to leave at 7:45 a.m. for an 8:00 a.m. class in San Beda's law grad school which I handle every few weeks.

The night before I spoke in an Arellano Law symposium on Taft where I was told that some of the attendees planned to be in People Power Monument tomorrow. Same thing I hear all over, like in the launch last Tuesday of an Ateneo re-issue of Tibo Mijares' Conjugal Dictatorship at the Bantayog ng mga Bayani, where desaparecido Tibo belongs. Along with Digong's Ma who I marched with in Davao, where he himself never figured in any anti-dictatorship activity I came to know of.

It is to Digong's credit that he has let us deplorable whiners alone, to air our grievances. No harassment. Also, looking back, I find myself thanking him for his moving Macoy's remains, furtively and disingenuously, to the Libingan, spawning questions from, and movements by, millenials.

Anyway, what follows are - My Edsa war stories of 1986 February 22 Lunch with Philip Kaplan, the U.S. charge, at the U.S. Ambassador # 39 Forbes residence. Philip Habib (Reagan' s special envoy) had just flown home. I was spokesman of Prez-elect Cory Aquino, who had told Habib, "I won, and I will take power." Nyet to power-sharing which Habib suggested, on Reagan's instructions.

I went to Cojuangco Bldg., our HQ. Eggie Apostol had called, worried for Manong Johnny, et al. (FVR was to follow later). Teddy Benigno called to tell me about the unexpected event unfolding at Edsa (Camp Aguinaldo).

Cory was in Cebu. Media in Manila and from abroad asked me: "What's going on?" Was it what the Reform the Armed Forces Movement told us the year before? That night, my wife, Dulce, and I drove around the Edsa camps. We saw little activity. We heard Manongs JPE and FVR, and later, Cardinal Sin and Butz Aquino. I did not get in, on advice that the Cory spokesman's presence could be mischaracterized. The appeal for help over Radio Veritas sounded genuine enough. Roy Golez and Justice Alampay had their electrifying defection announcements. I called Cebu. Miguel Perez Rubio said: all hands were safe. February 23.

We went to Sunday Mass early and shopped for the possible long haul ahead. I went back to HQ. Everyone I asked - Joker Arroyo, Raul Contreras, Ed Zialcita, et al. - said: "Thou shalt not go to Edsa. Possible zarzuela: you-never-know. Just remain at HQ as Cory, Jr. and not risk compromising her."

Later, I could stand it no longer. Cory had earlier planed back to Manila. I prevailed on Joker, to let me accompany him to EDSA. So off we went, along with my Dulce, and his Fely

Aquino, to Camp Crame. Butz was dozing off in a VW along Edsa. Mario Raymundo, my Pasig townsman, had the mic at the camp gate. Gen. Ed Ermita told me the Cory-Doy civilian component should move in. Power abhors a vacuum. Towards dusk, the tanks and APCs turned around, to the relief of the cheering throng. I saw Rod Reyes at eventide; he said, for Marcos, it was all over, echoed by foreign correspondents. Providence and the People had rescued the doomed putschists from being barbecued.*

February 24. June Keithley was a terrific bandida on Radyo Bandido. There was a very early morning cheering at the Cojuangco Bldg. The confetti canyons of Makati were agog at word that the Marcoses had fled, a false alarm, but, there was no stopping the tide of history. I joined Cory about mid-morning in the Wack Wack residence of a sister of hers. Over the objections of her security, Cory stubbornly insisted on speaking at Edsa, POEA Bldg., and had her way. Dulce joined Sid Hildawa in speaking there that afternoon.

Led by Cory and Doy, we met at his Mandaluyong pad, with Sen. Tanny Tanada, Ka Celing Munoz Palma (a Hall was named after her in QC last Saturday), Batasan members, et al.. We later moved to the home of Speaker Pepito Laurel nearby. By then, Channel 4 was ours. I drafted Proclamation 1, aided by Neptali Gonzales, Raul Gonzalez and Nick Jacob. I helped prepare EO No. 1. I also typed in a rinky-dink typewriter the unconventional Cory-Doy oaths of office, aided by Louie Villafuerte. (He earlier suggested to arm ourselves, as Marcos was capable of one last act of madness.") The installation was supposed to take place that evening at Club Filipino.

I had helped Mel Lopez and Monching Mitra ask Club management whether it would be willing to host the perilous affair. Everybody was gung-ho. The Directors were all at Edsa, led by Dr. Ramon Suter, the Club Prez, who said, through Marquitos Roces, "by all means, go ahead." I talked with Remedios Morco, the operations manager, to tell her that Cory might hold office there. Sure, she would give up her own office for her. Someone called to say the Club would be bombed: "Make our day, baby," we said. The personnel slept at Club to be around for the planned inauguration early the next day.

When the idea of a February 24 oath taking was junked, due to differences on venue - the military wanted it in a camp, but Cory persisted on a civilian facility - I went back to the Club to face the throng expecting to see Cory and Doy that night. As Cory Jr., I underwhelmed them. Some groused that they should have been consulted. But, no time. The event had assumed a life of its own. I didn't tell the throng the reason for the cancellation (the venue debate).

Back at Wack Wack, I had a meeting with Cory, Uncle Jovy Salonga, Jimmy Ongpin and Teddyboy Locsin. We picked the first Cabinet members. I went back to Doy's residence. MP Lito Puyat kindly lent me his driver and car. I went back to HQ. And then home to watch the pathetic Marcoses on TV. Unhinged, Macoy branded me (and one Ernie Salandanan] a Commie, seen raising a red flag in Laguna ha, ha.

February 25

Inauguration Day in Club. Cory had resisted the idea that the oath taking be held in a military camp. Manongs Johnny and Eddie showed up flashing the Laban sign and gamely sang Bayan Ko. The speech Teddyboy drafted the night before for Cory was missing; he rushed a new one along the lines approved and refined by her the night previous. We had lunch in Ruby Borja's Takayama Resto nearby. We saw on TV the Marcos rites in Malacanang, which were cut off.

That afternoon, the new Prez, at Wack Wack, named Joker executive secretary and me, her spokesman, still. Joker slumped in a chair. I looked down at my shoes a looooong time. We got a lecture on public service. Had there been a transition period, Joker and I could have escaped. We had not planned to join government. But, it was no time to say No.*

We "cracked" a code. Marcoses leaving! Steve Psinakis called from California to confirm they would be flown out. On TV Sec. George Shultz confirmed what the American envoy earlier relayed to Cory. Bye-bye.

As I had predicted in my presscons, there would be dancing in the streets by those asking what they could do for the country, ready to put themselves where their mouths were. That Edsa Spirit we want back. Sadly the People who Powered, asking what they could do for the country, not long thereafter, asked what the country could do for them.

That Evil Spirit we want exorcised. Forever. But our all too Brief Shining Moment lasted only till late 1987, in my view. And now we have as Prez one who did not take part in Edsa'86, to my knowledge.

May we not lose our moral stamina, the Tigulangs among us, now asked by millennials what happened in those four days of February when we shocked and awed the world. Jorge Santayana said, those who do not remember the past, are condemned to repeat it and that a nation without a memory is a nation of mad men. And as the ancients would say, those who the gods would destroy they first make mad. Queem deus vult perdere prius dementat.

Mad, sad and lonely. At the top.

The President's oath is to do justice to everyone. But the way he is personally throwing everything at Sen. Leila, including the kitchen sink, seems to loom as the Mistrial of the Millennium. Given what all-powerful Digong has been recklessly saying against Leila, he has kept dishonoring his vow to do justice to every man. So does the Justice Secretary, who also sadly misspeaks. And the SolGen. They are joined by the PNP chief who says he is ready to be her custodian. Ang dadaldal. The Prez is not in the business of prejudging. And we cannot have a Secretary of Injustice. Or an over-eager bridegroom for a SolGen. Or a clown for PNP chief. Yes, from where I sit, I discern or theorize the making of a Mistrial, warranting a nullification of what the administration has done to Lei. The charges she now faces should all be dismissed so that Never Again will he have a Prez who Prejudges and preempt the criminal justice system.

Digong is now the subject of SPO3 Arturo Lascanas, who may have flipped, but not flopped. Now the administration dismisses the poignant recantation of someone with intimations of mortality and it wants a probe, not of murders, but of perjury.

For crying out loud!

oooooo

34
Crimes Vs. Humanity
Everyone's Concern
Sep 29, 2016

All that PNP Top Gun Bato de la Rosa & Co. had to do was use the Internet to find out the drug situation in Colombia. No need to junket to verify whether the hardline bloody policy has failed there (and indeed, all over, such as in Thailand). He would have seen that Colombia Prez Juan Manuel Santos agonizes in explaining to a peasant why he is being prosecuted for planting marijuana whose use is legal elsewhere. Too much blood has been spilled in vain, it seems to me.

Maybe Foreign Affairs Secretary Jun Yasay has not heard of the UNIVERSAL Declaration of Human Rights (UNDR)? A predecessor, Carlos P. Romulo had a hand in its formulation. Jun has asked the world to let and leave us alone on allegations of UNDR violations.

And Prez Digs Duterte, Justice Sec Vit Aguirre and Sen. Manny Pacquiao may have no right, in my view, to sniff and condemn some of us as subhumans and therefore cannot have human rights? Bizarre. An apology cannot really undo the damage done by rashness.

The Prez should not apologize for mistakenly identifying an alleged criminal but for naming and shaming anyone at all in gross violation of due process and the presumption of innocence. Those he does not apologize to, tepok na: which investigating prosecutor and judge would shame him?*

Digs has dug up history. But, not deep enough, with all due respect. He may need to dig deeper as a would-be history buff. Now, he even blames God. Did he really attend Ateneo and San Beda?

Anyway, any clan reunion such as we had last Sunday for primo Benedictine Fr. Manuel Maramba, who turned 80, with HILARION Maramba-Henares present, is bound to be HILARIOUS, given his penchant for his last few millions words, if handed a mic. My eldest brod, Tony, would tell me about him in the late 50's, on TV. Kuya Tony idolized him and iconic Claro M. Recto more so.

I first heard Cuya Larry in some college (St. Paul?) program when I was in San Beda. Late 50's. Riveting, I thought. Last we talked at length was a few years ago, when he regaled me with tales of what he would do to quiet his raging hormones. He's going on 93; other members of our Thundering Herd would tell me Cuya Larry is a libido legend, but only in his own mind. Last

Sunday, he said he could tell Kamandag Manong Johnny Enrile "di ka nagiisa." Cuya Larry's Fables?

I don't know if he is anti-American but Cuya Larry and Manong have eloquently expressed faith in the Filipino. Pro-Pinoy, no question.

Another kin came over during the party and whispered that the Supreme Court would decide the Libingan ng Mga Bayani (LMB) case 10-5 in favor of the Non-Bayani. Tingnan natin kung ang kamaganak ko ay hindi bulaang propeta. I don't predict as we have up to this week to file our memoranda. I filed a brief paper last Tuesday for Rene, Sr. (me), Rene, Jr. and Rene III stating that the time had not yet come. Better to focus first on Rep. Harry Roque's bill to rename LMB to Libingan ng Mga Bayani at Pangulo. Lincoln is buried in Illinois but remains highly regarded all over the world for RESPECTING everyone. Great Golfer Arnie Palmer, also gone, but is fondly remembered for RESPECTING everyone. Who is fond of DISRESPECTING?

Anyway, safer to talk about the past. As long as Digong revives memories of the Massacres of Bud Dajo and Balangiga (its Bells I saw in Fort Warren just outside of Cheyenne in 1993; PNoy could have asked for their return, before signing EDCA), we should also recall the Chinese Massacres here of 1603 and 1639.

Digs' cunning Chinese hosts might remind him soon, when he visits China and asks for favors. You never know. To put him on the defensive, they may recount that like the fabled and vilified Jews, anywhere, here, the Chinese largely powered trade, labor, and industry in Spanish colonial economy. In spite of the economic benefits given by the Chinese, Spain viewed them with suspicion, fear, and, like we, Indios, do, or did, even with racial contempt (recall Hitler and Jewry).

Given the growing population of the Chinese, government severely restricted Chinese migration here and their businesses were heavily taxed.

By 1581, Guv-Gen Gonzalo Ronquillo de Penalosa created the Parian, for the Chinese in Manila to reside in, well within the range of Spanish cannons.

It became the business center of Manila. On the belief that gold was abundant here, Mandarins came on May 23, 1603, which convinced the Spaniards that a Chinese invasion was imminent, making them suspicious of those in the Parian. The overt hostility of the Spaniards alarmed the Chinese. With such mutual belligerency on both sides, actual confrontation was inevitable.

The Chinese struck on October 3, 1603, in Tondo and Quiapo. Responding Spanish forces were killed to the last man. The Spaniards called > in the Indios and the Japanese residents. (Indios also helped the U.S. in Bud Dajo.) The Chinese then retreated to San Pablo, where they were eventually overwhelmed by forces led by Cristobal de Axqueta Menchaca.

About 23,000 Chinese were massacred. Years later, Governor General Corcuera forced the Chinese to labor in Calamba, and the subsequent abuses committed by Spanish Bossings sparked the second Chinese rebellion. It began in Calamba on November 19, 1639 and spread to other towns in Laguna. The Alcalde Mayor of Laguna and several Spanish priests were killed, and municipal buildings and churches were burned to the ground. For three months the rebels fought in Laguna until they were driven to the mountains.

In February 1640, the Chinese rebel remnants surrendered to Guv-Gen Corcuera in Pagsanjan. Almost 20,000 had been killed.

What about the Muslims in recent times? On February 7 and 8, 1974, also around 20,000 Muslim, Christian and Chinese civilian residents of Jolo died in the the burning of the central commercial town caused by repeated land, sea and air bombardments by the lethal Marcosian war machine. They were caught in the crossfire in   the two-day battle of the AFP soldiers and the fighters of the Moro National Liberation Front (MNLF). It was characterized as, "the worst single atrocity" , which rendered scores of thousands Muslims, Chinese and Christians as homeless refugees. (Mamasapano, 44 heavily-armed attacking government troopers and who cares about the Muslim civilian victims?)

The two-day continued Philippine Navy (PN) battleships bombardments from the sea, and the Philippine Air Force (PAF) jet fighter planes,   T-28 `Tora-Tora'; warplanes and helicopter gunships bombardments and machine-gun firing from the sky led to the burning of the central Tulay mosque, Chinese Pun Tai Kung temple and the entire commercial town of Jolo. The foreign press exposed the laughter of defenseless and harmless civilians and the looting and ransacking of the Moro-abandoned houses by our soldiers.

The timid local press, quiet. But, I had known about the carnage in a reunion, of our Rizal Hi Class of '55. A classmate who attended the PMA and finished as No. 3 in his class said he took part in it.

We should not tell Digs what we think of his ancestors, may Intsik, may Muslim. Mabalasik. May dugong Waray pa. Masaya. Singing in After Darkin Davao City past midnight. No wonder.

If we cannot have what we like, we have to like what we have? War could be hellish but if we are to blame the Kanos for Bud Dajo and Balangiga, we must also recall what we did to our own civilian Muslim brothers and sisters.

Digs' hero, Macoy, isn't one to the Muslims and to many, who also matter. Last Monday, Digs inaugurated a 405-MW power plant, funded by a fellow Bedan, Andrew L. Gotianun, Sr., in Mindanao. The Bedan Mafia is all over the place. Where will the Mafiosis take us? To Paradise? Or where Digs tells fellow Bedan Leila de Lima to go? She is giving as good as she gets. Attagirl. But, I am saddened aren't I?

To lift me up, why not listen to Digs and Lei singing in duet, Something Stupid, of which, for some reason, I am often reminded these days.

More time Digs asks for. Let's give it. He will have enough rope to lead us to heaven, sana po, or hang himself with, huwag po naman sana. Presidential temperament should be higher than parochial or mayoral.

To Lei, what doesn't destroy you can only make you stronger. Don't get mad. Don't get even. Get ahead.

Better, Stronger, Together*.

oooooo

35

Healing & Killing
Sept. 21, 2016

It is plain wrong to mark September 21, 1972 as the notorious Day of Infamy. For me it was just another day in the office.

As head of the San Beda Free Legal Aid Clinic, I monitored from my Mendiola office a rally in Plaza Miranda, that Thursday, just in case I'd need to rush over. Ka Pepe Diokno, Charito Planas, Bal Pinguel, et al.. spoke. September 22, Friday, ho-hum, again, save that on my way home that night from San Beda, to our rented Sandejas, Pasay apartment, my Beetle radio announced the spurious ambush of Manong Johnny Ponce Enrile, who admitted the falsehood on February 22, 1986.

44 Septembers ago, when Macoy inflicted martial law, the following describes how I felt as an uhugin lawyer and saw other Panyeros/as like -

"The German lawyer [who] was . . .particularly prepared to accept as `law' anything that called itself by that name, was printed at government expense and seemed to come `von oben herab." L. Fuller, Positivism and Fidelity to Law - A Reply to Professor Hart, 71 Harv. L. Rev. 630, 659 (1958). "Hitler did not come to power by a violent revolution. .

The exploitation of legal forms started cautiously and became bolder as power was consolidated. The first attacks on the established order were on ramparts which, if they were manned by anyone, were manned by lawyers and judges. These ramparts fell almost without a struggle." Id.

Tañada, Diokno, Salonga, Ordoñez, Garchitorena, Arroyo, Gonzalez (Raul), Bobbit Sanchez, et al. were grossly outnumbered by the Fil-German types, as the ramparts fell with little struggle. So newbies such as the Jojo Binays, Odie Melchors, By Bocars, Ed Araullos, Boy Ellas, Jimmy Malanyaons, Jun Factorans, Boyet Fernandezes, Hessie Mallilins, and a few others, including myself, tried to fill in the breach. Macoy failed to heed the advice in Shakespeare's Henry VI on what take-over plotters should do: "The first thing we do, let's kill all the lawyers," in supreme tribute to those who would ask the foolish questions of the day, and hang the costs and consequences, and not let the ramparts fall without any struggle. (Of course St. Ives was a lawyer and yet became a saint, and the people were astonished.)

Ka Pepe organized the Free Legal Assistance Group (FLAG), after being detained from 1972 to 1974 without being charged! I joined. In 1980, some of us who thought lawyers should take public stands aside from traditional lawyering, formed MABINI (Movement of Attorneys for Brotherhood, Integrity and Nationalism, Inc.) but kept our warm ties with FLAG and iconic Ka Pepe. I am among the relics and antiques left, MD, Masamang Damo, marching again to the beat of a different drummer (Thoreau), taking the less travelled road (Frost), sailing against the wind (the Kennedys), and asking "why not?" while seeing things that never were (others may ask "why" , seeing things that are - GB Shaw).

We are now forming a new group, with new blood, while we watch what the quiet Integrated Bar of the Philippines, the Philippine Bar Association, the Philconsa, the big bufetes, and others will do in the wake of the extrajudicial executions far exceeding what happened in late 1972. Population reduced violently by 3,000 in weeks!

In the late 80's we were delighted to gain vocal support from interlopers Prez Jimmy Carter, State Asec Patricia Derian, Amnesty International, atbp. Pakialameros/ as.

In 1986, alien interference was capped by divine intervention. The world was shocked and awed by People Power, which saw the nearly bloodless end of the reign of a kleptocratic gross human rights violator who Digong idolizes and would now want him to rest with heroes. Digong should consult FVR, who the Marcoses put one over on, in 1993.

I am on the side of fellow Bedan Leila de Lima against fellow Bedans Vit Aguirre (our hardworking colleague in the case of Hubert Webb) and Digong Duterte (with whose courageous principled Mom I marched in Davao after Ninoy was salvaged). I was flabbergasted to see Vit acting like the Speaker or Committee Chair of the House he seemed to own last Tuesday. Usually, outside counsel is not much more than part of the furniture, while the elected lawmakers dominate and scintillate.

Of course litigators walk through with their witnesses on their testimony. And no lawyer should ask a question the answer to which he doesn't already know, particularly on cross. Trial Technique 101.

Speaker Bebot Alvarez, who may or may not remember me, is sounding like a Certified Tuta.

Vit and Digong should stop naming and shaming people and instead just file cases against them, particularly the wealthy and well-connected. Not enough to increase the body count of the poorest of the poor who should be rehabbed, with better planning. Packed prisons depress and convert humans into brutes.

I am comfy with underdogs. Sen. Dick Gordon took ousted Lei's place. I trust him if only cuz ang hambog galit sa kapwa hambog. He can stand up to Digs, on principle. When Erap kicked Dick around so needlessly in 1998, I assisted him against my Canvassing client Erap. Dick told me that some Jesuit taught him that "in this world, the world laughs with you but, you weep alone." As a human being, Christian and lawyer, I say, "if you need me and you have no one else, you'll never walk and weep alone. I'll walk and weep with you, if you will allow me." When Erap fell from overdog to underdog, I finally heeded his request to join his legal team. I walked and wept with him, along with his friends and wives. I entered my appearance and joined his formidable battery but an accused goes to bat with two strikes against him. Like beleaguered Sen. Leila. Hang in there, Lei! I admire your moral stamina. Let's see what Vit will do with the names you supplied as elements of the alleged Davao Death Squad.

There is no substitute for due process and no hardline bloody policy has succeeded anywhere in the world. If there is money to be made, the failed drug policy won't erase trafficking in which Dona Josefa Marcos engaged while teaching in Arellano High School, and arrested by top cop Telesforo Tenorio, according to Tibo Mijares in the Conjugal Dictatorship. Tibo disappeared while his teenaged son, Boyet, was sadistically salvaged.

I see a ray of hope in Imee's seeking forgiveness for his Pop's abuses and am appalled by Bongbong' s insult of the human rights victims as only after money. No wonder, poor unknown Leni G. Robredo beat him, and fellow Bicolanos Alan (by marriage), Chiz, Gringo and Sonny, splitting the votes with the Oragons while billionaire BB had his Solid North. Feisty Leila is also Bicolana.

The voters could have chosen a Healing Prez. But a plurality preferred a Killing One, who gives the rich due process but spares few in unkind naming and shaming. Traffic, after 80 days of Digong is much worse in Metro Manila. What if he and Bato de la Rosa execute ten "resisting&quo t; scofflaw drivers? A remedy worse than the disease.

Sec. Vit Aguirre can just file charges, if he has the evidence, against Lei and others named and shamed. He should recall how our common client, Hubert Webb, was named and shamed, tried and convicted by publicity, early on, and spent more than 15 years in jail for something I then said I'd carry to my grave he did not commit. He was thousands of miles away but the hooting throng carried the day.

Obsta principiis. Resist the first encroachments.

Oh, yes, kudos to Ted Locsin, who may share with Digong a liking for the dirty finger sign, but the communications guys can always explain they only mean to say, "you are No. 1." The spin I gave in 1986., if my memory is true.

oo0Ooo

36
Why I Publish/Reprint Books

Tatay Jobo Blizes
Self-Publisher

Writings are timeless and they act as mirrors to history. I publish writings as they remain relevant anytime. I have seen a lot of good writings in the internet, in magazines and newspapers. But most writers have only one or two articles and therefore not enough material to be published as a book. And yet, many of them need to be published or archived. There are also writers who write a lot but never publish them. There are also old books with no more prints available. The solution is to publish/reprint.

I do this for free because of the print-books-on-demand (POD) system, but the printed or hardcopy is not free

The printed book will always be there among your collections or libraries. Not all use the internet. The internet access has its technical problems. I can produce fiction, non-fiction, in color also.

My booklist can be seen at http://tinyurl.com/mj76ccq (copy and paste)

Permission had been granted by the author/authors to print their books under my free self-publishing service. They own copyrights to their works.

Interested reader may request free reading of any of my books, articles or essays via online reading or ebook. Just email me.

Thank you.

ooooo